A Sense of Urgency:

Legalizing Online

Initiative Petitions

700,000 PETITION SIGNATURES

Title: A Sense of Urgency:
       Legalizing Online Initiative Petitions

Copyright © 2014, 2015
This is the 3rd Edition, 2017

ANOTHER GOOD DAY WITH GOD,
PUBLISHING

Messages to the Publisher/Author of this Book can be posted at:

LastChancePetition.com
CaptainPetition.com

ISBN 10: 0991610776
ISBN 13: 978-0-9916107-7-8

I Give Thanks to
My Very Good Friend

GOD

the Creator of
the Universe
Who Inspired Me to
Complete this Book

Inclusions and edits in previous 2nd Edition :

A suggested preliminary amount of handwritten signatures was included into the first Example Initiative Petition "a", requiring Petitioners to get a minimum ___100___ handwritten signatures before being allowed to post their Initiative Petition Online, so as to reduce the amount of persons posting Initiative Petitions compulsively; of course, the amount can be changed to a different amount, such as ___1000___, et cetera.

A suggested amount of time was included into the first Example Initiative Petition "a", requiring Online Initiative Petitions to be posted for a minimum ___2___ months before getting online signatures, to allow comments from the public; this will allow the Petitioner to review comments and edit the Initiative Petition before the Public begins signing the Initiative Petition;

Example Initiative Petition "J", now says that the entire US Government can not give any money to foreigners without Voter Approval; previously it was limited to the US Executive Department.

Inclusions and edits in this current 3rd Edition :

Example Initiative Petition "N" in the appendix calling for the possible disbandment of Germany has been edited because of recent historical evidence presented to the Author that many communist gypsy jews in various countries such as England, France, Poland, Russia, and the United States, orchestrated the harassment of the financially successful homogeneous Caucasians who were residing in Germany at the time, that eventually led to WW1 part 1, and WW1 part 2 (a.k.a. WW2).

Included a suggested Petition in the appendix at "Q", to raise the Voting Age Limit to 47.

CHAPTERS

APPENDIX : EXAMPLE PETITIONS

a	Legalizing Online Initiative Petitions
A	Legalizing the word "GOD"
B	Stopping the US Debt Crisis
C	Stopping State Debt
D	Vote about Wars
E	Freedom of Assembly
F	Judicial Department Improvement Act
G	State Transportation Improvement Act

H	**Graffiti Law**
I	**Law about Prisons**
J	**Money to Foreigners**
K	**Food Labels**
L	**Marijuana**
M	**US Spying prohibited**
N	**Liberating Germany**
O	**Free Ticket to Africa for Emancipated negroes**
P	**Imprisoned negroes**
Q	**Other Suggested Initiative Petitions**

APPENDIX : OTHER

R	**Memorandum from California Secretary of State that prevents Electronic Signatures (only on Initiative Petitions)**
S	**Personal Letter sent to California Governor Jerry Brown, and four State Legislators, about Legalizing Online Initiative Petitions (Oct 2011)**
T	**List of States that allow Initiative Petitions**

1

1

The US government is a dictatorship

1

News Flash !

The United States Government is a Dictatorship !

The reason the United States Government is a Dictatorship Government, is because the Public Voters can not easily change a Law.

The Law is what controls the Public Voters.

To change a Law, the Public Voters need to put a proposed Law onto the Public Ballot, to be voted for, or against, but at the moment, the Public Voters can not do that easily.

And the Public Voters also can not easily tell their minority group of elected legislators to vote for, or against, a Law.

And therefore, to change a Law, thousands of Public Voters have to rally together, and waste alot of time and money, each and every time the Public Voters want to put one Law onto the Public Ballot, and every time the Public Voters want to try to get their minority group of elected legislators to do something.

Not very many people have alot of time and money to try to get thousands of signatures to get a Law onto the ballot, or to try to tell their minority group of elected officials to do something.

Since it is very difficult for the Public Voters to change a Law themselves, and since it is the Law that controls the Public Voters, and since the only persons who can easily change the Law are the minority group of US citizens that calls itself the Government, all means that the Public Voters are being controlled by a Dictatorship Government, or at the very best, a Democratic-Dictatorship Government.

And over the years, it has not been very difficult to convince those persons voluntarily employed in the Government, that *the US citizens have almost no control over their Government*.

As a result of the Public Voters having almost no control over their Government, *many of the persons employed in the US Government and the State Governments of the US, are seldom brought to trial or punished for their misdeeds, and tend to be swindlers*.

As a result of the US Government being filled with corruption, and incompetents, the US Government tends to constantly put the US into more Debt, constantly gives tax payer money to foreign militaries, foreigners, and whomever they want to give the tax payer money to, and constantly gets the US into pointless and costly Foreign Wars, Et Cetera.

1

If the Public Voters have to spend years of their time just to rally together to get something **URGENT** onto the ballot, just so they can tell their corrupt US Government to do something, or not to do something, each and every time **the Public Voters need to stop their own Government from doing corruption**, then that is not much of a Democratic Country, because not very many people in the US want to spend several years to try to get something onto the ballot, even if it would mean telling their corrupt US Government to do something, or not to do something.

And even if the Public Voters did get something onto the ballot, and even if the Public Voters did vote for and approve their own Law, then what happens if that same Law needs to be amended later ?

The Public Voters probably would need to spend years rallying together again to amend their own Law !

And it also seems that a voter can't get their elected minority group of Legislators to do anything without a major contribution or bribe.

For example, if you telephoned your minority group of federal and state legislators, and told them about a Good Law that you wanted to be enacted, or about a Law that needs to be amended, then that minority group of elected legislators will probably ignore you.

That is the reason the Citizens of the United States have a Dictatorship Government!

To correct this dire situation, *the Public Voters need to take the time to propose a Law that legalizes Online Initiative Petitions !*

I will say it again...

URGENT:

***The Public Voters
need to take the time
to propose a Law that
legalizes Online
Initiative Petitions in
their State,
if the Public Voters
ever want to Control
their Dictatorship
Government !***

See the next Chapter !

2

2

Online
Initiative Petitions

ANOTHER GOOD DAY WITH GOD

How many of you have heard about an Initiative Petition, or what an Initiative Petition is ?

2

An Initiative Petition is a Proposed Law, and is usually proposed to the Public by one or more Voters who are trying to get their Law put onto the Ballot, so that all of the other Voters can vote for, or against, their Proposed Law.

Initiative Petitions can propose a State Law, a County Law, or a City Law.

At the end of this book in Appendix "T", is a list of States that allow Initiative Petitions.

You may want to telephone your local Library, and ask how you can do an Initiative Petition in your State, to get a State, County, or City Law onto the ballot.

After a Voter files their Initiative Petition with the appropriate State, County, or City Clerks, the Initiative Petition usually needs to be circulated (passed around town) to be signed by thousands of other Voters, within a certain amount of time, with valid signatures, so the Initiative Petition can get put onto the ballot.

Volunteers, or paid Petition Circulators, will then walk around town asking thousands of registered Voters to put a valid signature onto their copy of the Initiative Petition that they have with them.

Extra signatures will need to be collected, because not all signatures will be valid.

An Initiative Petition is one of the most powerful items in a Democracy, but not all States allow the Voters to collect signatures on Initiative Petitions.

At the end of this book, is a list of States that allow Initiative Petitions.

You may want to telephone your local Library, and ask how you can do an Initiative Petition in your State, to get a State, County, or City Law onto the ballot.

And as far as the amount of paper needed... if one page attached to a copy of your (paper) Initiative Petition can hold 20 signatures per page, and if you need **10,000 to 500,000 (valid) signatures**, then you will need alot of paper and alot of time to get those **10,000+ to 500,000+ signatures**.

It will be so much easier, and less expensive, if you could post your paper Initiative Petition online for other Voters to sign online.

2

An Online "Signature" can consist of something as simple as a username and password. (An Online "Signature" is also called an "Electronic Signature".)

An Initiative Petition is a very powerful Petition, and is about the only way for the Public Voters to tell their Dictatorship Government what to do, and therefore, there probably will be a small army of Government Servants in that US Dictatorship Government, who will try to stop you from legalizing Online Initiative Petitions.

Warning: There are many corrupt persons in the Dictatorship US/State/County/City Governments, who do not want the Voters to control them.

For example, toward the end of this book in Appendix "R", is a copy of a memo from the California Secretary of State, that prevents Electronic Signatures from being used only on Initiative Petitions.

The memo was issued by the California Secretary of State even though many Laws in California specifically allow the California Government to accept Electronic Signatures.

The memo is an example of how only one State Employee acted as a dictator, and used their government job to prevent several million other Voters from being able to easily put a Law onto the ballot using Electronic Signatures.

And California is only one example of a State that needs an Online Initiative Petition Law.

Another example, not included in this Book, is the written **Opinion No. 12-80, from the Tennessee Attorney General, dated Aug. 2, 2012**, that invalidates a Tennessee Law called "UETA" (Uniform Electronic Transactions Act), when the Law is applied to the use of Electronic Signatures on Initiative Petitions; the written Opinion discusses any possibly indecisive wording used in the "UETA", and then interprets the wording in a manner that is more restrictive against the Voters, and thereby probably contradicts the entire purpose of "UETA"; it can be presumed that the Tennessee Attorney General would not hesitate to take the issue to a dictator judge.

Warning: Your first Initiative Petition should be done in paper, and it should be a Statewide Initiative Petition to Legalize Online Initiative Petitions in your State !

2

See the first example in the Appendix "a", for an example of a Statewide Initiative Petition, to be done on paper, that will Legalize Online Initiative Petitions in your State !

Even though Online Initiative Petitions may not be illegal in your State, if you posted an Online Initiative Petition in your State, without Legalizing Online Initiative Petitions first, then one of the Dictators in your State probably will take the whole issue to a corrupt Court, and then, a corrupt Judge will probably invalidate the thousands of electronic signatures you collected on your Online Initiative Petition.

You have been forewarned!!!!!!!

See the first example in the Appendix "a", for an example of a Statewide Initiative Petition, to be done on paper, that will Legalize Online Initiative Petitions in your State !

The first example in Appendix "a", provides an outline for a (paper) Initiative Petition that will Legalize **Online Initiative Petitions** in your State, if you if reside in a State that allows you to circulate your own Initiative Petitions; you have permission to copy and modify the example Petition.

An Initiative Petition can be used for many things, and can be for something as simple as a j-walking Law, or for something more complex, such as for one of the many example Initiative Petitions in the Appendix of this book.

An Initiative Petition can be used to :
* legalize or prohibit something
* repeal something
* get someone onto the election ballot
* remove someone from their government job (with or without reason)
* pardon someone, or reverse a pardon
* increase or decrease the sentence of someone who has been convicted of something
* indict someone to court

With Online Initiative Petitions, the Public Voters can easily control their Government.

Many simple and complex clauses can be put into Initiative Petitions, and the following three Chapters explain three very powerful "Clauses" that you can put into all of your own Initiative Petitions, so the Public Voters can effectively control how their Government must respond to your Law after your Law is approved at the ballots.

2

Note about collecting Signatures: the most cost-effective way to collect Signatures on a paper Initiative Petition, may be to ask dozens of volunteers to collect Signatures throughout the work week at their permanent addresses, and then you can advertise those locations using radio, fliers, mailers, etc..

Warning: Even though your Proposed Law can be as simple as a j-walking Law (that you intend thousands of Voters to sign), you may want to optionally consult with other persons who are also interested in your Initiative Petition, such as a volunteer attorney service, a paralegal, the public law librarian, or other persons who will give free legal advice, and who can review and edit your Initiative Petition, and who can double check that your Initiative Petition does not conflict with existing laws, and does not have any loopholes; your public library may be able to assist you in locating some of these free legal services.

Warning: To supersede prior Laws, you may want to actually include into your Proposed Law a clause that specifically says that your Law will supersede any conflicting provisions that are in any prior enacted Laws, to the extent allowed by Law.

If you reside in a State that does not allow you to collect signatures on an Initiative Petition directly from the other Voters, then you may want to:

2

* pester your State Legislators with letters and telephone calls demanding that they enact a State Law that allows you to do Direct Initiative Petitions in your State, for both Paper and Online Initiative Petitions, and/or,

* collect informal signatures, on an informal Petition, to be given to your State Legislators, that asks them to Legalize both Paper and Online Initiative Petitions.

At the end of this book, is a list of States that allow Initiative Petitions.

Just as there were not very many persons who signed the Declaration of Independence in the United States, there will not be many persons interested in preparing an Initiative Petition to collect signatures to legalize Online Initiative Petitions, however, many of those non-participants will still sign the Initiative Petition if prepared by someone else.

The Signers of the US Constitution instituted a representative form of "government" probably because of the lack of telephones, roads, and cars 200 years ago; nowadays, the residents of the "Colonies" can now take more direct control over the "government" by using Initiative Petitions and Online Initiative Petitions.

3

3

The
"Control Your Congress"
Clause

You heard it here first !

The "Control Your Congress" Clause.

3

An Initiative Petition proposed in your State is a powerful way to supersede and control your minority group of State Legislators, County Legislators, and City Legislators, but what about your minority group of Congressional Legislators ?

At the moment, an Initiative Petition can only propose a State Law, County Law, or a City Law, and there are no official Initiative Petitions for the Voters to use to directly propose a Federal Law (at the moment).

If you want to propose or change a Federal Law then you need to: ***Do a Statewide Initiative Petition that Proposes a State Law, that specifically tells the Congresspersons of your State what to do while they are in Congress !***

Don't ask them to do something !
Tell them to do something !

The State Voters in your State can enact a State Law that tells the State Congresspersons of your State what to propose, and what not to propose, and what to vote for, and what not to vote for, while they are in Congress; it is that simple, but beware, there will be opposition.

I will not be surprised if some Congresspersons and Judges somewhere start saying that the Voters are not allowed to enact any Laws that tells the minority group of elected Congresspersons what to do while they are serving the Voters in Congress !

A full-text example version of this Powerful "Control Your Congress" Clause is as follows below.

You will need to put the Clause directly into the text of your proposed Law.

The Clause is to be included as a part of your Law, and is not intended to be a Law in and of itself; the Clause is just one Section of your Law; for example, when the example Clause below refers to "this State Law", the Clause is referring to the entire State Law, and not just one Clause.

The Appendix of this book, has many Example Initiative Petitions with this powerful Clause included into the text of the Initiative Petitions.

(free to copy and modify)

3

THE "CONTROL YOUR CONGRESS" CLAUSE

The Duties of the US Congresspersons of this State, pertaining to this State Law, are as Follows:

Each person elected by the citizens of this State, who are elected to serve this State in the Congress of the United States of America, whether as a Senator or a Representative, shall immediately work together during their terms of office, and propose or maintain similar Bills, in both houses of Congress, calling for:

(for example...)

* calling for an Amendment to the United States Constitution to include [such and such Amendment]

* calling for an Amendment to the United States Constitution that includes the same text as Parts A, B, C, and D of this State Law (not included in this example Clause) but not Part F

* calling for an Amendment/Repeal of a particular Federal Law or Federal Regulation.

And whenever the Majority Vote in One of the Two Houses of the United States Congress Votes against the proposed Bill, then all the State's Senators or Representatives, elected for that respective House of Congress, shall Propose the same Bill again to the appropriate House Committee, and shall continue proposing the same Bill to the appropriate House Committee, indefinitely, whenever a Majority Vote in that House of Congress Votes against the proposed Bill.

3

[If this Law is calling for a Constitutional Amendment...] Whenever the US Congress approves the Constitutional Amendment as described in this Law, and then returns the Constitutional Amendment to the State Legislature of this State for their Vote, then the State Legislature shall approve of the Constitutional Amendment unless the Amendment is different from what is proposed in this State Law, and in that situation, then the State Legislature shall give the Constitutional Amendment to the Voters of this State for their Approval.

3

If any Federal Judge rules by
Court Decision, that the Voters of
this State do not have the Right to
tell the Congresspersons of this
State what to Vote for or Against
in the United States Congress,
then the Congresspersons of this
State shall indefinitely propose
and vote for the impeachment and
removal from office of that
Federal Judge.

If any Congressperson of this
State does not obey this Section of
this Law, then any Grand Jury of
this State may indict that accused
person for violating this Section of
this Law, without any Statute of
Limitations being imposed on the
violation ;

when a Grand Jury in this State indicts the accused person, a felony arrest warrant shall be issued the same day as the indictment ;

after conviction, and during sentencing, the convicted person shall be sentenced for a minimum of 4 years in the State Penitentiary, without parole, and a maximum of life in the State Penitentiary, without parole ;

after conviction, the convicted person shall not be permitted to be an Employee of any State or Local Government in this State ;

the Voters may also do a State Initiative Petition to indict or impeach that person, without Statute of Limitations being imposed, for violating this State Law ;

such a Vote at the ballots can be done regardless if a Grand Jury decides not to indict that person ;

3

the Voters may also do an Initiative Petition to increase or decrease any sentence imposed by a Judge or Jury against the convicted person ;

the accused person may be indicted, impeach, or receive a greater or less sentence, with a minimum 70% majority Vote at the ballots.

This Section of this State Law, shall remain in effect until all Constitutional Amendments, as described above in this Section, are enacted, however, the parts of this Section that calls for an indictment of any Congressperson of this State who disobeys this State Law, and the parts of this Section that calls for the Removal of Office of a Federal Judge, and the parts of this Section that Prevents the Congresspersons of this State from Voting for any Bill Contrary to this Section and this State Law, shall remain in effect indefinitely.

The Congresspersons of this State shall also support any other US Bill proposed by the Congresspersons or Legislatures of another State that accomplishes the same purpose of this Section.

The Congresspersons of this State
shall also Vote against any Bill
proposed in the United States
Congress that contradicts the
purpose of this Section or that
contradicts any Laws enacted
pursuant to this Section.

[end of "Control Congress"
clause]

3

ANOTHER GOOD DAY WITH GOD

4

The "Who should interpret this Law" Clause

You heard it here first !

The "Who should Interpret this Law" Clause.

4

The "Who should Interpret this Law" Clause, is a powerful Clause that you may want to put into your Initiative Petitions.

This Clause specifically designates who is legally allowed to Interpret your Law after your Law is approved by the Voters at the Ballot.

A full-text example version of this Powerful "Who should Interpret this Law" Clause is at the end of this Chapter.

Before the introduction of this powerful Clause (in this book), Courtroom Judges would be the persons who would interpret any Law that needed to be interpreted during any particular Court Case, and the interpretations being done by one Judge in one Court Case could be changed by another Judge in another Court Case.

Often, it is a coin toss about how a Judge will interpret a Law, and an interpretation of any particular Law may often be done by a corrupt Judge.

And in actuality, when a Law is "interpreted", then the Law is Amended, because it has the same effect, and in My opinion, the Judicial Department does not have the Constitutional Authority to Amend Laws.

This Powerful "Who should Interpret this Law" Clause needs to be put into more Laws, because not very many people want a small group of corrupt Judges to Amend Laws that were enacted by several million Public Voters or by several hundred Legislators.

There have been many instances where those Judge Amended Laws (also called Judicial Prudence, and Judge made Laws), blatantly have not Declared what the Law or the Public Voters actually want from that Law.

I will not be surprised that when you put this Powerful Clause in an Initiative Petition, then many Dictator Judges will probably try to invalidate the Clause.

However, if the Public Voters persistently demand that they want this Clause, then I believe that this Clause will persevere.

There can be several different versions of the "Who should Interpret this Law" Clause; for example, the Clause can be modified to apply to Federal, State, County, or City Laws, and to Federal, State, County, or City Legislators.

4

Note: An Interpretation Clause may not need to be put into each every Initiative Petition after a Law is enacted that contains a general Interpretation Clause to cover all Laws, such as the general Interpretation Clause that is in the Example Initiative Petition in Appendix "F"; however, even when a general Interpretation Law is enacted, you could still do a specific Interpretation Clause to discuss items not discussed in the general Interpretation Clause, but each Interpretation Clause would be subject to the other, and therefore, their provisions would probably need to mention the other and be worded so as to avoid possible conflict or confusion between the two.

Until a general Interpretation Law is enacted that covers all Laws, I suggest just putting an Interpretation Clause into each Initiative Petition; and then, after a general Interpretation Law is enacted later, any conflicts or confusion that exists between your specific Interpretation Clause and the new general Interpretation Law can be clarified with amendments to one or both of the Interpretation Clauses.

The full text version of this Powerful "Who Should Interpret this Law" Clause is as follows:

(free to copy and modify)

4

THE "WHO SHOULD INTERPRET THIS LAW" CLAUSE

For the purposes of this enacted Law, any Interpretation of this Law will also be considered an Amendment of this Law, and except as otherwise expressly permitted in this Clause, this enacted Law may only be Interpreted, Amended, or Repealed, with the final Approval of the Voters.

If any part of this enacted Law needs Interpretation by any Court within the State, then such an Interpretation may be done by the Court for the purposes of allowing the Court Case to continue.

The Court shall then send all the Interpretations sought by the Judges and the Parties in the Court Case to the State Legislature for their Interpretation.

If any Party in the Court Case is not satisfied with the Interpretation that was done by the Judges, then the parts of the Court Case needing the Interpretation shall be postponed, and shall wait for the Interpretation to be done by the State Legislature.

If any part of this Law needs Interpretation by any other Government Agency in this State outside of a Court Case, or by any State Congresspersons outside of a Court Case, or by any Federal Government Agency outside of a Court Case, then such an Interpretation shall be done by the State Legislature, and shall not be done by any Court.

After the State Legislature Interprets the Question of Law, the State Legislature shall give the Question of Law along with Interpretations sought, to the Voters at the next General Election.

4

If all the Parties in a Court Case, are not satisfied with the Interpretation that was done by the State Legislature, then they may all agree to postpone the Court Case and wait for the Interpretation to be done by the Voters.

All Court Cases pending when the Voters answer the Question of Law, shall use the Interpretation of the Voters.

Any Government Agency or State Congressperson who seeks an Interpretation directly from the State Legislature outside of a Court Case, need only wait for the Interpretation of the State Legislature before acting on the Interpretation, *however, when the Voters answer the Question of Law, then the Government Agency or State Congressperson shall be subject to the Interpretation of the Voters.*

4

The State Legislature shall also publish the Names, Public Addresses, and Interpretations, of each of the Judges, members of the State Legislature, or other Government Employees, that had a personal Interpretation that was offered to the State Legislature for this Law.

Any Interpretation required to be done by the State Legislature in this Section shall be done within 1 month.

[end of "Interpretation" clause]

Note: the italics in the "Interpretation" Clause above is optional when put into an Initiative Petition; the optional italics portion allows the interpretation to proceed from the Legislators to the Voters for an Interpretation, however, sending the Law to the Voters for an interpretation will require more time, and therefore...

* you may want to include the italics into more important Initiative Petitions, such as Tax Laws, or Laws telling State Congresspersons what to do, etc, so the Voters can immediately interpret the Law;

* you may want to omit the italics from less important Initiative Petitions, such as for j-walking Laws and other traffic laws, so the Voters will not be asked to interpret every Law in the Law Books; if necessary, the Voters can still amend or repeal those minor Laws later with an Initiative Petition.

5

Paying the Bill:

The "Campaign Reimbursement" Clause

You heard it here first !

The "Campaign Reimbursement" Clause.

5

Since your first Initiative Petition will be a Paper Initiative Petition that will Legalize Online Initiative Petitions in your State, you probably will be spending several thousand dollars for printing costs, circulation costs, storage costs, et cetera.

Perhaps you would like to get reimbursed.

If you include a "Reimbursement Clause" into your Proposed Law, then you will get reimbursed after your Proposed Law is enacted by the Public Voters !

The full text version of this Powerful Clause is as follows:

(free to copy and modify)

5

THE "CAMPAIGN REIMBURSEMENT" CLAUSE

The People of this State, thank the several People who volunteered and risked their money to fund this Campaign for this Law, that enabled 500,000 signatures to be Collected so this State Law could be put on the November Ballot, and therefore, the People of this State agree to repay the persons who talked directly to the Proponent of this State Law, about how they wanted to be reimbursed for their contributions pursuant to this Clause, and who then funded this Campaign for the following expenses:

(1) the wages of the Circulators who personally collected Signatures from the Public, not to exceed the State minimum wage per person employed unless the person employed was a professional security guard for hire who collected the Signatures;

(2) the rent paid, if any, that was used to rent the places where the petitions were being signed;

(3) the print-shop costs of printing and preparing the Petition for Signatures;

(4) the costs of Radio Advertising, Billboard Advertising, Mail Advertising, and Handbill Advertising;

(5) the wages of the Proponent and Staff, not to exceed the State minimum wage per person employed, unless the person was employed with a professional qualification, such as a Lawyer.

5

All such Applications seeking Reimbursement of Costs Paid shall be supported with Receipts and with Affidavits under the Penalties of Perjury; two State Employed attorneys employed within the State Legislative Department shall draft the Affidavits for Applicants to sign.

A Reimbursement Office appointed by the State Legislature shall review the Applications seeking Reimbursement, and then repay the approved Applications pursuant to this Section within 1 year after receiving the Receipts and Affidavits, and shall continue to do so for all persons not paid until 2 years has past from the date this Law was enacted.

To be eligible for reimbursement, all such persons submitting an Application, Receipts, and Affidavit to the Reimbursement Office, also needs to be on the list of persons who contributed to this Campaign, as recorded by the Proponent during the Campaign for the purpose of reimbursing contributors to the Campaign.

The Reimbursement Office shall only give reimbursements to approved Applications if the Applicants are on the list of contributors provided to the Reimbursement Office by the Proponent.

5

[end of "Reimbursement" clause]

APPENDIX
OF
INITIATIVE PETITIONS

(All are free to Copy and Modify)

a

Example Petition:

Legalizing
Online
Initiative Petitions

State Law

ANOTHER GOOD DAY WITH GOD

Preamble of the Law.

This Law makes it easier for the Public Voters to Circulate, Review, and Sign any State, County, or City Initiative Petition, because all Initiative Petitions filed in this State, will also be filed online at an Online-Site that is supervised by the same State Clerk who is normally responsible for registering all State Initiative Petitions circulated by a Public Voter.

This Law also makes it easier for the Public to Register to Vote, because the burden of Registering to Vote will be done automatically every time the Public Renews their State Identification Card or State Driver License.

This Law also makes it easier for the Public to Vote at the Ballots for your Initiative Petition, because this Law enables the Public to use their State Identification Cards, or State Driver Licenses, as their official Voter Identification Cards.

This Law is for YOUR benefit.

We the People thank GOD for this Law.

PART A. THE STATE EXECUTIVE DEPARTMENT SHALL MAINTAIN AN ONLINE SERVICE FOR INITIATIVE PETITIONS.

For the purposes of this State Law, an Initiative Petition, is a State or Local Initiative Petition to:

1. Enact, Repeal, or Change a Law,
2. Recall a Government Official from Office with or without reason,
3. get someone put on the ballot for an Election,
4. grant or reverse a pardon,
5. increase or decrease a Court sentence of someone,
6. get a Court retrial, and/or
7. Indict someone to Court.

For the purposes of allowing the State Residents to easily sign and un-sign Initiative Petitions, the State Executive Department shall within 1 year after the Enactment of this Law, begin operating a functioning Online Site to accomplish the purposes of this Law, pertaining to the Public being able to post and sign Initiative Petitions Online.

ANOTHER GOOD DAY WITH GOD

For the purposes of regulating the integrity of the Electronic Signatures that are put onto Initiative Petitions, only the State Executive Department is allowed to maintain an official Online-Site for the purposes of Collecting Electronic Signatures Online for any Initiative Petition that has been approved for Statewide or Local Circulation within this State.

For the purposes of this Law, whenever an Initiative Petition is approved for Circulation by the appropriate State, County, or City Clerks, then the State or Local Clerks shall ensure that the Initiative Petition is posted Online at the Site maintained by the State Executive Department.

The Online-Site maintained and regulated by the State Executive Department must at a minimum :

a. Be accessible by all the appropriate State, County, and City Clerks, for the purposes of allowing those Clerks to Count and Validate all the Electronic Signatures of the Registered Voters that reside in their Jurisdictions;

b. Be accessible by all the appropriate State, County, and City Clerks, for the purposes of allowing those Clerks to Post any Statewide or Locally Circulated Initiative Petition at the Site;

c. Allow all the Initiative Petitions posted at the Site to be viewed online for free, by any person, without the person needing to sign-in to the Site to view the Initiative Petitions that are posted at the site;

d. Allow any Registered Voter to sign-in at the Site, using a simple Username and Password to sign-in at the Site, for the purposes of allowing the Registered Voter to sign and un-sign Initiative Petitions Online at the Site;

for the purposes of obtaining a Username and Password, any Registered Voter may obtain in person only, after the providing a sufficient amount of personal information to prove their identity, a temporary Username and Password at any designated location, as designated by the appropriate State, County, and City Clerks; the personal information provided shall at a minimum be the same personal information that the appropriate Clerks would need to Validate Handwritten Signatures on Initiative Petitions; after obtaining a temporary Username and Password, any Registered Voter shall be allowed to change their Username and Password as many times as they want at the Online-Site free of charge;

e. Allow any Registered Voter who has successfully registered to sign-in at the Site, to sign and un-sign any Initiative Petition Online at the Site, as many times as they want to, however, the State Executive Department may require that all Electronic Signatures that are put onto or removed from those Initiative Petitions to be done within the Official Time Period for Collecting Signatures for any particular Initiative Petition;

f. Allow any qualified person to post and remove Initiative Petitions at the Site according to the Initiative Petition rules, free of charge;

BEFORE ANY INITIATIVE PETITION WILL BE POSTED ONLINE, THE PETITIONER MUST FIRST OBTAIN __100__ VALID HANDWRITTEN SIGNATURES, USING A PEN OR PENCIL, along with any other information that is required by the appropriate Clerks to validate the handwritten signatures; the handwritten signatures must be from persons who are eligible to sign Initiative Petitions in that jurisdiction;

if the telephone number of the signers are provided by the signers, then the appropriate Clerks must telephone a signer if the Clerks are not able to verify the handwritten signature provided by the signer;

within __14__ days after being submitted by the Petitioner, the Clerks must verify the handwritten signatures provided;

if __100__ of the handwritten signatures are valid, then the Clerks shall post the Initiative Petition online, to allow any eligible person to comment, sign, or un-sign the Initiative Petition online;

g. Have two online Comment pages for any Initiative Petition filed, to allow anyone to post a comment or question about the Initiative Petition; the Comment pages must be accessible by anyone without needing to sign-in to the site to post or view the Comments;

one Comment page will accept comments "for" the Initiative Petition, and one Comment page will accept comments "against" the Initiative Petition; each Comment page can be divided into smaller pages when the Comments are many;

any spam comments that are removed by the Clerks, must be put into a separate page titled "Comment Page spam" and must viewable by the Public;

ALL INITIATIVE PETITIONS POSTED ONLINE, MUST BE POSTED ONLINE, AT THE DESIGNATED ONLINE-SITE, FOR A MINIMUM OF _2_ MONTHS, FOR THE PURPOSES OF ALLOWING THE PETITIONER TO ACCEPT COMMENTS POSTED ONLINE AT THE DESIGNATED ONLINE-SITE, BEFORE VOTERS CAN BEGIN SIGNING THE INITIATIVE PETITION;

DURING THAT _2_ MONTHS, THE PETITIONER MAY EDIT THEIR PETITION; THE PETITIONER IS ALSO ALLOWED TO SPECIFY A LONGER AMOUNT OF TIME, TO ACCEPT COMMENTS FOR LONGER THAN THE MINIMUM _2_ MONTHS;

THE PETITIONER IS ALSO ALLOWED TO SPECIFY THAT THE PETITIONER WILL "ACCEPT COMMENTS UNTIL FURTHER NOTICE" TO ALLOW THE PETITIONER TO ACCEPT COMMENTS FOR AN UNSPECIFIED AMOUNT OF TIME PAST THE MINIMUM _2_ MONTHS;

THE PETITIONER IS ALSO ALLOWED TO EXTEND THEIR PETITION AND COMMENT PERIOD PAST AN ELECTION PERIOD.

PART B. COUNTY CLERKS TO MAINTAIN DROP BOXES FOR INITIATIVE PETITIONS; FORM OF INITIATIVE PETITIONS.

Section 1 of 2. County Clerks, or other appropriate Government Clerks, to maintain Drop Boxes and Online Service for Collecting Signatures.

For all the Initiative Petitions filed with any County Clerk, or other appropriate Government Clerk, who will be responsible for Counting the Signatures that are put onto the Initiative Petitions, the Clerk shall maintain __1__ or more Drop Boxes for Collecting Signatures on the Initiative Petitions being circulated;

the Clerks must provide to the Public Voters, small Pre-Printed Paper Forms or Cards, that each Contain one Unique Title for each of the Initiative Petitions being circulated, one Place for the Signers to provide their voter information and Signature, and a notice that the voter information and Signature must be on file with the Clerks before the Clerks will accept the Signature as valid;

the Clerks may maintain more than __1__ Drop Box at different locations throughout their Jurisdiction, such as putting __1__ or more Drop Boxes at the Public Libraries and the Post Offices, as a convenience to the Public;

in addition to the required Drop Boxes, the Clerk may also use a functioning Kiosk, to Collect Electronic Signatures; the minimum required Drop Box(es) must be located at the same location as the Clerk.

All Service Fees pertaining to maintaining the Drop Boxes, Pre-Printed Forms or Cards, and Kiosks, as discussed in this Section, shall not be charged directly to the Proponents of the Initiative Petitions, and shall not be charged directly to the Signers of the Initiative Petitions.

Section 2 of 2. Method of Writing, Collecting, and Validating Signatures, for Initiative Petitions.

All State and Local Laws enacted pursuant to the State Constitution pertaining to Initiative Petitions, must forthwith be liberally construed to allow the following:

a. Any type of Handwritten Signature or Electronic Signature can be used to sign any Initiative Petition, however, all Signatures must be on file with the appropriate Government Clerk to be considered valid; and the appropriate Government Clerks must file and update the Handwritten Signature or Electronic Signature when offered by the Voter, and must allow the Voter to have more than One Signature on file, such as the Signature on their Identification Card, along with a Signature that they want to use to Sign Initiative Petitions.

b. The heading and other basic wording of an Initiative Petition can be in any Format, however, the Format of any Initiative Petition must give sufficient notice to the Public as to what the Petition pertains to, and the appropriate Government Clerks must be able to Verify the Signatures on an Initiative Petition and that the Signatures are for that Initiative Petition, however, the State Legislature or another Government Agency are allowed to provide suggestions to the Public as to various Formats that may be used by the Proponents; This Provision of this Law is to allow Initiative Petitions to be accepted by the appropriate Government Clerks regardless of Format used, if the Format is Legible and allows the Public to easily Distinguish the Initiative Petition as being an Initiative Petition.

c. Initiative Petitions also need not contain the Full Text of the Initiative Petition when Signed, need not be Attended when Signed, can be Circulated by Anyone who is Eligible to Vote or Not, can be Filed by Any Proponent who is Eligible to Vote or Not, does not need to have the Signatures Certified by the Proponents or the Circulators working for the Proponents, can be Signed by the Voters using any method desired by the Proponents and the Voters such as in person or by mail or by telephone or by fax or Electronically, and a Signature on an Initiative Petition is prima fascia evidence that a Voter was willing to Sign the Initiative Petition as it was presented to the Voter.

d. Proponents shall not be charged a fee to file an Initiative Petition with any Government Agency before being allowed to Circulate the Initiative Petition for Signatures, and shall not be charged a fee by any Government Clerks to Verify the Collected Signatures, and shall not be charged a fee to have an Initiative Petition put onto the Ballot after the required amount of Signatures are Verified by those Clerks.

e. The responsible Government Clerks shall review all Initiative Petitions submitted for approval for circulation, as directed by the State Legislators, for the purposes of categorizing each Initiative Petition, and checking for duplicate or very similar Initiative Petitions; and when two Initiative Petitions are similar, then the proponents shall be notified by the Government Clerks, by mail or e-mail as directed by the proponent, and within an amount of time as directed by the State Legislators, asking each proponent if the proponent wants to continue with their submitted Initiative Petition, or withdraw their submitted Initiative Petition.

When enacting State Laws, the State Legislature shall ensure that all State Laws comply with this Law, unless the enacted State Law is Approved by the Voters.

For the purposes of this Law, if an Initiative Petition is left unattended by a Proponent or Circulator, a sufficient means must be provided to prevent Signatures from being removed from the Initiative Petition and to prevent the Initiative Petition from being tampered with.

For the purposes of this Law, whenever an Electronic Signature is Collected, an Electronic means must be provided for the Signer to check what they Signed, and an Electronic means must be provided for the Signer to remove their Electronic Signature from the Initiative Petition they Signed; such a means need only be provided until the Official Time that the appropriate Government Clerks stop accepting Collected Signatures. [a]

For the purposes of this Law, the main criteria used by the appropriate Government Clerks when Validating a Signature, is that the Handwritten Signature, or Electronic Signature, and any other required Legible Voter Information, must be on File with the Clerks, so as to enable those Clerks to Verify that the Signature is for a particular Voter, and to Verify that the Signature is for a particular Petition.

PART C. FEEDBACK SYSTEM TO PUBLIC FOR INITIATIVE PETITIONS THEY SIGNED.

When the Government Clerks do a final Count of the Collected Handwritten and Electronic Signatures put onto an Initiative Petition, the Clerks shall maintain an Online Electronic File that Contains an Extract of all Signatures that the Clerks Validated, and an Online Electronic File that Contains an Extract of all Signatures that the Clerks did not Validate.

The Extracts put into the Online Electronic Files can be as simple as the Voter Card Numbers of the Signers, or a Secondary Voter Card Number provided to the Signers for signing Initiative Petitions; the Filenames of the Electronic Files must contain the Name and intended Ballot Year of the Initiative Petition.

Any Extract used by the Clerks shall be in such a format that does not disclose the Identity and Address of any Signer, but in such a format that will allow the Signers to Identify themselves and what they Signed.

The only purpose of the Extract is to allow the Signers to Verify what they Signed and did not Sign, before and after the Clerks publish an Official Count of the Signatures put onto an Initiative Petition.

Prior to the Clerks publishing their Official Count of Signatures, the Clerks must display the Online Electronic Files for a minimum of _1_ month, as Publicly Viewable Electronic Files;
and during that time the Public shall be allowed to Inspect and Verify what they Signed and did not Sign, and during that time, the Clerks must promptly Update the Online Electronic Files when the Clerks Change the Validity of any Handwritten Signature or Electronic Signature put onto an Initiative Petition.

After the Clerks publish their Official Count of Signatures for an Initiative Petition, the Online Electronic File of Extracts shall be:

a. Permanently available Online to the public for free Download, regardless if enough Signatures were Collected to put the Initiative Petition on the Ballot or not, without the public needing to sign-in to the site.

b. Published in Paper Format, for free, for any Public Library located in the same County or City that the Clerks have Jurisdiction in, upon request of the Public Library, and when Published for Free, various Formats can be used for the Published Paper Version, such as using 7pt type with 7 Columns per page.

c. Published in Paper Format, for a fee, for any person who requests a Copy, and the cost for such a copy shall not exceed the cost for the Paper and Ink used to make the Copy, and shipping Costs.

PART D. DRIVER LICENSE CAN BE USED AS VOTER IDENTIFICATION CARD; AUTOMATIC REGISTRATION TO VOTE.

Section 1 of 2. State Driver License or State Identification Card to be Voter Identification Card.

Drivers Licenses, AND Identification Cards, can be used by State Residents as their Voter Identification Card.

The State shall not charge a fee to anyone to issue them a State Identification Card.

Section 2 of 2. Automatically Registered to Vote; Contents of Voter Registration Card.

The State Legislature shall enact State Laws that determine:

a. how to automatically Register people to Vote when they obtain a State Driver License OR a State Identification Card.

b. how any new State Residency Waiting Periods, if any, will be imposed before the person can vote, and if those Effective Dates will be printed on the Cards.

c. how any "Eligibility to Vote" status, will be printed on the Cards.

d. how the State will send the State Driver License Information AND the State Identification Card Information to the appropriate Government Clerks of the City and County of Residence of the Card Holder.

e. how the State will update Information Sent to those County and City Clerks when the Card Holder reports a change in Residence.

f. what other contents shall be printed on a State Identification Card or State Driver License, such as, for example, City, Zip, County, and Voting District.

All mailed communications done with the Voter, by any State or Local Government Agency, pertaining to issues arising from or pertaining to this Law, shall be done using the Mailing Address as reported by Voter, and, the Mailing Address of the Voter may be a Post Office Box;
whenever any mail is mailed to the correct address of the Voter on file, using a mailing that requires a signature of the Voter, and if the mailing is returned to sender, then a second mailing must be mailed to the Voter using standard mail that does not require a signature, saying that the State or Local Government Agency may have unclaimed mail that belongs to the Voter.

PART E. ENACTMENT OF LAWS PURSUANT TO THIS LAW; TIME TO COMPLY WITH THIS LAW; INTERPRETATION OF THIS LAW; PAYING THE PROPONENT OF THIS LAW.

Section 1 of 4. State Legislature shall Amend or Repeal other similar Laws.

The State Legislature shall amend or repeal all prior State Laws, to the extent allowed by the State Constitution, to conform with this State Law.

Section 2 of 4. Time for State Legislature to Enact Laws; Time for Clerks to Comply.

Pursuant to this Law, the State Legislature shall enact all the required State Laws, required by this Law, before the next General Election.

The appropriate Government Clerks shall fully conform to this Law before the next General Election.

Section 3 of 4. Amending and Interpreting this State Law.

(Put Chapter 4 here - the Interpretation Clause)

Section 4 of 4. Paying the Bill.

(Put Chapter 5 here -
the Reimbursement Clause)

* * * *

THE FOLLOWING ARE THE SIGNATURES OF THE REGISTERED VOTERS WHO WANT THE ABOVE INITIATIVE PETITION PUT ONTO THE BALLOT

1. Name/City/State/Signature:

2. Name/City/State/Signature:

3. Name/City/State/Signature:

4. Name/City/State/Signature:

5. Name/City/State/Signature:

6. Name/City/State/Signature:

7. Name/City/State/Signature:

8. Name/City/State/Signature:

9. Name/City/State/Signature:

A

A

Example Petition:

Legalizing the word "GOD"

US Constitutional Law

ANOTHER GOOD DAY WITH GOD

(free to copy and modify)

Preamble of the Law.

This Law is being made because of recent events in Court Cases where Judges have not been allowing people to use the word "GOD".

A

We the People thank GOD for this Law.

Section 1 of 5. Legal to say the word GOD.

Any person, including Federal, State, or Local Government employees, who are in their official capacity or not, can use the word "GOD", or any reference to "GOD", in any written or spoken communication.

Each State in the United States need not prohibit by Law, Public or Private Prayers, or Discussions, involving "GOD", from being voluntarily spoken, voluntarily repeated, and voluntarily heard, in any Public or Private Institution.

Each State in the United States, and the United States Government, is permitted to require phrases or speeches, involving the word "GOD", to be spoken or signed, by any hired, appointed, or elected Government Employee, as a requirement for holding office.

Section 2 of 5. Interpretation of this Law by US Voters.

If any part of this Law needs Interpretation by a Federal Court in the United States, after any part of this Law is enacted to be an Amendment to the US Constitution, then such an Interpretation shall be asked to be done by the Voters of the United States, and shall not be done by any Federal Court in the United States.

Section 3 of 5. State Congresspersons to Petition for Passage of this Law.

(Put Chapter 3 here - Control Your Congress Clause)

Section 4 of 5. Amending and Interpreting this State Law.

(Put Chapter 4 here - the Interpretation Clause)

Section 5 of 5. Paying the Bill.

The People of this State, thank all of the Participating Churches that helped put this Law onto the Ballot, and agree to Reimburse all the Participating Churches for the amounts shown on all of their Receipts, for any Moneys they Paid to help put this Law onto the Ballot, and the State Legislature shall write the check that Reimburses any Participating Church, within 4 months after receiving a Copy of the Receipts from a Church, provided however, that the Church must be recorded on the List of Participating Churches who helped put the Law on the Ballot, as recorded by the Proponent during the Campaign.

A

* * * *

**THE FOLLOWING ARE THE SIGNATURES
OF THE REGISTERED VOTERS WHO WANT
THE ABOVE INITIATIVE PETITION PUT
ONTO THE BALLOT**

1. Name/City/State/Signature:

2. Name/City/State/Signature:

3. Name/City/State/Signature:

4. Name/City/State/Signature:

5. Name/City/State/Signature:

6. Name/City/State/Signature:

7. Name/City/State/Signature:

8. Name/City/State/Signature:

9. Name/City/State/Signature:

B

B

Example Petition:

Stopping the
National Debt Crisis

US Constitutional Law

(free to copy and modify)

Preamble of the Law.

The United States Government will always say they need more money, irregardless of how much money they are already getting, and then they will often increase the National Debt as a result.

B

At the moment, the US National Debt is over 19 Trillion Dollars ($19,000,000,000,000) according to the following two sites:

* www.usdebtclock.org

* www.nationaldebtclocks.org/debtclock/unitedstates

The US National Debt is over 19 Trillion Dollars because the US Congress Incessantly Borrows and Spends Money, and because of the Interest on that Money Borrowed; of that 19 trillion dollars, the most recent 17 trillion dollars was "borrowed" within the previous 15 years.

This Law simply says that the United States Government can not increase the National Debt in times of peace, and must limit their spending to what they are already getting, unless the Voters Allow an Increase to the National Debt.

We the People thank GOD for this Law.

PART A. THE NATIONAL DEBT LAW.

Section 1 of 4. US Government not allowed to increase National Debt.

All persons, including all persons employed in the United States Government, are prohibited from increasing the National Debt of the United States.

Section 2 of 4. Exceptions.

An exception to increasing the National Debt is with the Explicit Approval of the Voters of the United States, obtained with a minimum 70% Majority Vote of the Voters of the United States.

Another exception to increasing the National Debt is when any war is officially declared by the US Congress, and when such a war is officially declared, then the US Congress may increase the National Debt to such an extent to accomplish the war, however, if the United States is not being actively and openly attacked on US soil during such a War, then the US Congress must get a minimum 70% Majority Vote from the Voters of the United States to increase the National Debt to fund the War.

B

Any request to the Voters of the United States to increase the National Debt, shall specify the dollar amount sought, and explicitly itemize what the money will be used for.

Section 3 of 4. Interpretation of this Law by US Voters.

If any part of this Law needs Interpretation by a Federal Court in the United States, after any part of this Law is enacted to be an Amendment to the US Constitution, then such an Interpretation shall be asked to be done by the Voters of the United States, and shall not be done by any Federal Court in the United States.

Section 4 of 4. Penalties.

Any person who raises the National Debt in violation of this Law is Subject to being prosecuted for the crime of Felony Theft, according to the Laws of each State of the United States, for stealing money from the Residents of each State in the United States, and therefore, the accused person may be prosecuted up to 50 times, wherein each State Attorney General of each State in the United States each has a legal right to prosecute the accused person once in their State;

and for the Purposes of this Section, the accused person may only be prosecuted in a State Court, and shall not be prosecuted in a Federal Court;

and for the Purposes of this Section, an accused person need not be a Congressperson of the United States Congress to be prosecuted, and can be any person who is a Government Official or not;

and for the purposes of this Section, a Congressperson, or any other Government Official, shall be allowed to continue their official duties in Public Office, until they are Convicted in one or more States;

and for the purposes of this Section, the duty of an accused Government Official to defend themselves in the Criminal Case being brought against them by one or more State Attorney Generals, shall take priority over other Duties of the Government Official.

Each accused person, after being Convicted of their Felony Crime in one State, or more than one State, shall then be personally financially liable to every State in the United States for any National Debt they increased, and therefore, one or more State Attorney Generals, may each do a separate Class Action Civil Lawsuit against each Convicted person on behalf of the Residents of their State, to obtain the portion of any Money that was Stolen from the Residents of their State by the Convicted person, and upon successfully prosecuting the Class Action Civil Lawsuit, the Personal Money obtained from the Convicted person shall be reimbursed to the Residents of the State according to the Laws of the State.

B

If any person raises the National Debt not consistent with the exceptions stated in this Law, and if one or more State Attorney Generals files Formal Criminal Charges against the accused person in their State Court, and if the United States Federal Government obstructs justice by preventing the accused person from being prosecuted, or from being removed from office after being Convicted, then all the Governors of all the States in the United States, each has the right to issue an Executive Order that allows the Residents of their State, to postpone all Federal Tax payments, without any interest or penalty being due on the postponement until the Federal Government complies with this Law.

For each Congressperson that raises the National Debt not consistent with the exceptions stated in this Law and who is then Convicted for their Felony Crime in a State Court, fleeing from Justice, or Removed from Office:
the State Legislature of the State that elected that Congressperson, shall appoint from the members of that State Legislature, a temporary Congressperson to fill the vacant position of the Congressperson for the remainder of the term of that Congressperson.

PART B. DUTIES OF STATE CONGRESSPERSONS; INTERPRETATION OF THIS LAW; PAYING THE PROPONENT OF THIS LAW.

Section 1 of 3. Duties of State Congresspersons.

(Put Chapter 3 here
- the Control Your Congress Clause)

B

{ Also include the following... }

Until a US Constitutional Amendment is enacted pursuant to this Law: each person elected by the citizens of this State, who are elected to serve this State in the Congress of the United States of America, shall be prohibited from increasing the National Debt inconsistent with this Law, and shall vote against any Congressional Bill or other Congressional Act that Increases the National Debt, unless such an Increase to the National Debt is done pursuant to the exceptions specifically stated in this Law; and when such an exception is sought, then the aforestated 70% Majority Vote as required by this Law, shall be obtained from the residents of this State before the Congresspersons of this State will be allowed to vote for the increase of the National Debt in the United States Congress; and when this Law is disobeyed by the Congresspersons of this State, then the penalties of disobeying this Law will be limited to being prosecuted in this State, for doing a State Felony Theft; and furthermore, when this State Law is disobeyed, the State Governor will not be authorized to issue an Executive Order allowing the State residents to postpone their Federal Tax Payments.

Section 2 of 3. Amending and Interpreting this State Law.

(Put Chapter 4 here - the Interpretation Clause)

Section 3 of 3. Paying the Bill.

(Put Chapter 5 here
- the Reimbursement Clause)

* * * *

B

THE FOLLOWING ARE THE SIGNATURES OF THE REGISTERED VOTERS WHO WANT THE ABOVE INITIATIVE PETITION PUT ONTO THE BALLOT

1. Name/City/State/Signature:

2. Name/City/State/Signature:

3. Name/City/State/Signature:

4. Name/City/State/Signature:

5. Name/City/State/Signature:

6. Name/City/State/Signature:

7. Name/City/State/Signature:

8. Name/City/State/Signature:

9. Name/City/State/Signature:

C

C

Example Petition:

Stopping
the State Debt

State Law

(free to copy and modify)

Preamble of the Law.

The State Government will always say they need more money, irregardless of how much money they are already getting, and then they will often increase the State Debt as a result.

C

This State Law simply says that the State Government can not increase the State Debt and must limit their spending to what they are already getting.

And to help the State Government to reduce the State Debt, this State Law forces the State Legislature, when it wants to Increase the State Debt, to Explain why they can not Save for an Expenditure, and why they Can not Reduce the Wages of State Employees to pay for the Expenditure.

Also, to help the State Government to reduce the State Debt, this State Law forces the State Legislature to review the possibility of dividing a Fiscal Budget into 52 smaller Weekly Budgets, and to review Alternate Salary Systems to pay State Employees.

This is a State Law, and therefore the Voters will be able to propose Amendments to this Law with Less Signatures, compared to Amending a Provision of the State Constitution.

We the People thank GOD for this Law.

Section 1 of 5. State not allowed to increase State Debt without approval of the Voters.

The State Government of this State can not increase the State Debt, nor can anyone else increase the State Debt, without a minimum 70% Majority Vote from the Voters of this State.

ANOTHER GOOD DAY WITH GOD

As an alternative to raising the State Debt, the State Government shall:

a. Save for any particular Expenditure.

b. Reduce the wages of various Government Employees, beginning with the highest paid Government Employees and ending with the lowest paid Government Employees.

c. Reduce the Employment Hours of Various Government Employees, without laying anyone off.

d. Reduce the Amount of hiring done of New Government Employees.

Any request by the State Government to the Voters of this State to obtain money for any Purpose, and thereby increase the State Debt, shall specify the dollar amount sought, and what the money will be used for, and why the State Government can not pay the Expenditure by Saving for it, Reducing the Wages of Employees, Reducing Employment Hours, and Reducing the Amount of New Hiring done.

C

Section 2 of 5. State Legislature to review Alternate Salary Systems to pay State Government Employees.

To Aid the State Government in not raising the State Debt, the State Legislature shall review the possibility of implementing different Salary Systems to be used to pay State Employees, and then, the State Legislature shall:

* Publish an Official Report on its findings of such a Review, and

* Propose to the Voters, as necessary, any amendments to the State Constitution that are needed, and any amendments to other State Laws, if proposals are necessary, to enable the State Legislature to enact a New Salary System based on its findings.

For example, the State Legislature may want to:

* Install a Lower Base Pay System, for all State Employees, similar to a Minimum Wage.

* and then, allow for an increase of various Salaries of various State Employees in any given month or year, based on what the General Fund allows; e.g., the State's General Fund for this Fiscal Year had enough Funds to allow all the State Government's Minimum Wage Salaries to be paid in full, plus a 10% Salary Increase, and for the previous Fiscal Year, it was a 12% Salary Increase, however, some of the Salaries for some of the State Employees, for both Fiscal Years, were not allowed to increase more than 7% above the Government's Minimum Wage, as Set by the State Legislature, and therefore those particular State Employees only got a 7% Increase in their Salary above the Government's Minimum Wage.

C

The State Legislature may also want to install an IOU system for those years when the State's General Funds are low, for example...

* A State Employee is suppose to get paid $150,000 a year, but the General Fund only allowed $50,000, however, the $50,000 amount is still $25,000 above the "Minimum Wage" set by Law for that position, and therefore, the State Employee would be paid $50,000 and then get an interest free I.O.U. for $100,000, to be paid in a Subsequent Year when the General Fund allows it; getting paid according to this provision would just be a part of the job.

Section 3 of 5. Reducing the Debt.

The State's Fiscal Budget shall also be adjusted to pay a minimum of __1%__ of the State's Debt each year.

Section 4 of 5. Amending and Interpreting this State Law.

(Put Chapter 4 here - the Interpretation Clause)

Section 5 of 5. Paying the Bill.

(Put Chapter 5 here
- the Reimbursement Clause)

* * * *

D

D

Example Petition:

Right to Vote about War

US Constitutional Law

(free to copy and modify)

Preamble of the Law.

This Law allows you to take part in the United States Government declaring Offensive Wars and Defensive Wars.

This Law, will prevent the United States Government from offensively attacking a Foreign Government that is not attacking the United States until the United States Government gets the Approval of the Voters first.

D

This Law also forces the United States Government to get a periodic Vote from the Voters, if Safe to do so, about the Continuation of any declared Offensive War or Defensive War.

This Law also prevents the United States Militia from being Stationed in Times of Peace in any Foreign Country against their Laws or Customs.

We the People thank GOD for this Law.

PART A. DEFINITION OF WAR.

For the purposes of this Law, an Offensive War, or a Defensive War, is a War declared against any Foreign Government, or against any Foreigner or group of Foreigners.

For the purposes of this Law, an Offensive War also includes Offensive Attacks, that are done covertly or non-covertly, against any Foreign Government, or against any Foreigner or group of Foreigners.

For the purposes of this Law, Offensive Attacks also include any Offensive Attacks that are done covertly or non-covertly, as a means of imposing or enforcing any type of Domestic or International Sanctions, against any Foreign Government, or against any Foreigner or group of Foreigners.

For the purposes of this Law, Offensive Attacks also include any Offensive Attacks that are done covertly or non-covertly, as a means of thwarting any possibly possible threats that are seemingly being imposed on the United States by any Foreign Government, or by any Foreigner or group of Foreigners, whether or not the threats that are seemingly being imposed are marginally real, or persistently being perceived in a delirious state of persistent paranoia.

For the purposes of this Law, an Offensive War, or Defensive War, involves any type of Warfare Activity within the scope of Warfare;

and for the purposes of further defining Warfare Activities, from what is already defined in this Law, the United States Congress shall define what Activities are Warfare Activities, and what Activities are not Warfare Activities, when such Warfare Activities are performed by the United States Government, or against the United States.

D

For the purposes of Declaring a War against a Foreign Person, the term Foreign Person may include a Domestic Person, or Domestic Persons, in times of Domestic Civil War.

PART B. DECLARATION OF OFFENSIVE WARS.

Only a minimum 70% Majority Vote of the Voters of the Several States in the United States of America, can authorize an Offensive War.

The United States Government, can not declare an Offensive War against any Foreign Government, or against any Foreigner or group of Foreigners, without first obtaining a minimum 70% Majority Vote of the Voters of the Several States in the United States allowing such an Offensive War or Offensive Attack; and if the Voters approve of such an Offensive War or Offensive Attack, by a minimum 70% Majority Vote, then United States Government shall yearly thereafter obtain a minimum 70% Majority Vote of the Voters of the Several States in the United States allowing such an Offensive War or Offensive Attack to continue, if the United States Government wants to continue the Offensive War or Offensive Attack.

PART C. DECLARATION OF DEFENSIVE WARS.

Immediately After Declaring any Defensive War against a Foreign Country, or any other Persons or Group of Persons, Foreign or not, the United States Government shall immediately ask all the Voters of the Several States, if such a Defensive War shall continue, and then, if the Voters approve of the continuation of the Defensive War, by a minimum 70% Majority Vote, then United States Congress shall ask the Voters yearly thereafter if the War shall continue, and during each yearly Vote, the United States Congress will need a minimum 70% Majority Vote of the Voters to allow the Defensive War to continue.

D

PART D. DECLARATION OF SANCTIONS AGAINST A FOREIGN GOVERNMENT.

Only a minimum 70% Majority Vote of the Voters of the Several States in the United States of America, can authorize a Sanctions against any Foreign Government, or against any Foreigner or group of Foreigners.

The United States Government, can not declare any Sanctions against any Foreign Government, or against any Foreigner or group of Foreigners, without first obtaining a minimum 70% Majority Vote of the Voters of the Several States in the United States allowing such Sanctions;

and if the Voters approve of such Sanctions, by a minimum 70% Majority Vote, then United States Government shall yearly thereafter obtain a minimum 70% Majority Vote of the Voters of the Several States in the United States allowing such Sanctions to continue, if the United States Government wants to continue the Sanctions against the Foreign Government, or against the Foreigner or group of Foreigners.

PART E. DISAPPROVED WARS.

If a minimum 70% Majority Vote is not obtained from the Voters of the Several States allowing any Declared War to Continue, then the United States Militia shall immediately retreat from that War, and any such retreat shall be completed within 30 days or less, and any such retreat, shall be completely to the outside of the Foreign Country that the War was taking place in;

D

any such retreat shall be done, as far as practical, with a daily notice to those being retreated from, that a retreat is taking place, and that the United States Militia is exiting the Foreign Country, and that the United States Militia will not fire unless fired upon.

PART F. DISAPPROVED FOREIGN SANCTIONS.

If a minimum 70% Majority Vote is not obtained from the Voters of the Several States allowing any Foreign Sanctions to Continue, then the Foreign Sanctions shall be discontinued.

PART G. POSTPONING VOTE.

The United States Congress may postpone getting any Votes required by this Law, only if the United States is being openly and actively attacked on United States Soil to such an extent as to prevent the Voters from safely Voting, and if such a postponement occurs, then the United States Congress shall postpone getting the Votes only until it is Safe to do so.

PART H. UNITED STATES MILITIA STATIONED IN FOREIGN COUNTRIES.

The United States Militia is not allowed to station Troops in a Foreign Country without approval of the United States Congress, and the United States Congress shall have complete control of the time limits of such stationing of Troops.

Unless a Declaration of War is Publicly Announced against a Foreign Country, or unless a Post-War Resolution is being Enforced against a Foreign Country, the United States Congress is not allowed to station Troops in any Foreign Country that has as its Foreign Laws, or Popular Customs, provisions that forbid such stationing of United States Troops in that Foreign Country.

For the purposes of stationing Troops, any such inquiry done by the United States Congress about the Foreign Laws and Popular Customs of a Foreign Country pertaining to stationing United States Troops in that Foreign Country, shall non-inclusively include talking to various, non-partial Lawyers or Equivalents, who are not employees of that Foreign Country, so as to not limit any inquiry to only talking to the Government Employees or Government Diplomats of that Foreign Country.

D

This Part of this Law is to reduce Foreign Disputes against the United States, and to reduce possible Wars against the United States, that may arise as a direct result of the United States Militia blatantly violating the Foreign Laws, or Popular Customs, of any particular Foreign Country.

For the purposes of this Law, the term Foreign Country shall be applied to any group of persons claiming to be a Country, regardless if the group of persons is internationally recognized as being a Country, if the group of persons has a population greater than the least populated Country that is internationally recognized as being a Country.

PART I. INTERPRETATION OF THIS LAW AS A UNITED STATES LAW.

If any part of this Law needs Interpretation by a Federal Court, or Federal Government Agency, in the United States, after any part of this Law is enacted to be an Amendment to the United States Constitution, then such an Interpretation shall be done by the United States Congress who shall answer the Question of Law for the purposes of allowing the Court Case to continue or allowing the Government Agency to act on the Interpretation, and then the United States Congress shall give the Question of Law to the Voters of the United States along with all Interpretations sought by the United States Congress.

If the Court Case is not resolved at the time the Voters answer the Question of Law, then the Federal Court shall use the Interpretation done by the Voters.

PART J. DUTIES OF THE CONGRESSPERSONS OF THIS STATE.

(Put Chapter 3 here
- the Control Your Congress Clause)

PART K. AMENDING AND INTERPRETING THIS STATE LAW; AMENDMENTS; PAYING THE PROPONENT OF THIS LAW.

Section 1 of 2. Amending and Interpreting this State Law.

(Put Chapter 4 here - the Interpretation Clause)

Section 2 of 2. Paying the Bill.

D

(Put Chapter 5 here
- the Reimbursement Clause)

* * * *

E

Example Petition:

The Voters
Interpretation
of
Freedom of Assembly

E

US Constitutional Law

(free to copy and modify)

Preamble of the Law.

At the moment, the First Amendment is as Follows:

Congress shall make no Law respecting an establishment of religion, or prohibiting the free exercise thereof; or abridging the freedom of speech, or of the press; or the right of the people peaceably to assemble, and to petition the Government for a redress of grievances.

E

This Law clarifies and/or expands, the First Amendment of the United States Constitution, in your favor.

Congress has passed oppressive Federal Laws that discriminate against the majority, and prohibit your "freedom not to assemble" with any person based their race, color, religion, sex, or national origin, political affiliation, sexual orientation; these oppressive Federal Laws force you to assemble with the minority groups who you may prefer not to associate with.

Those Federal Laws are in direct violation of the First Amendment, because it may force you to assemble with people you do not like.

Isn't it obvious, especially with the "sexual orientation" part of their oppressive Federal Law, that the US Congress is often not capable of enacting Good Laws, and doesn't it call into question what Religion those people have ?

The white founders and white shop owners in the white colonies of the 1700's would be appalled at forced assembly in their shops and elsewhere, and would retaliate with petitions, and musket fire if necessary.

This Law protects Citizens of this Country, both while working and while not working, and this Law says that the Citizens of this Country can Assemble with whomever they want to Assemble with, at while working and while not working.

This Law prevents the US Congress from forcing you to assemble with people you do not want to assemble with, in your pursuit of happiness.

This Law protects your Right of Assembly.

We the People thank GOD for this Law.

140

PART A. FREEDOM OF ASSEMBLY.

Section 1 of 3. Right of the People to Assemble.

The US Congress, and the States, shall make no Law respecting the right of the people peaceably to assemble or not assemble, with people of their choice, for any legal activity of the people's choosing.

The US Congress, and the States, shall not force you to assemble or not assemble with other persons, during whatever legal activity you are doing, while working or while not working, if you do not like their:

E

* race,
* color,
* sex,
* national origin,
* political affiliation,
* religious orientation,
* sexual orientation,
* attitude.

Legal activities, as described in this Law, include, but are not limited to:

* running a business,
* choosing who you want to hire and fire,
* choosing who you want to rent or sell an apartment or house to,

* choosing who you want to be in a local privately owned community,

* choosing who you want to employ to buy, sell, or rent your private property,

* choosing who you want to assemble with on your property, based on their beliefs, such as, their religious or political beliefs.

Exceptions to this Law, include, instances of when Law Enforcement, or other Government Employees, such as Food Inspectors, are conducting their official business, and this Law, also does not necessarily apply to Persons who are Legally Confined by Law Enforcement.

This Law also does not necessarily apply to employee-to-employee relations for those persons employed within the Government as the Government is conducting its official business, although, the US, State and Local Governments shall not hire people who admit they have Homosexual Orientations.

Section 2 of 3. Duties of the States After Enactment.

After this Law is enacted into the United States Constitution, the States Legislatures of the several States, may establish State Laws, about how people, such as business owners, and those people who rent out property, shall File with the State and Local Governments for Public Inspection, any General Public Notices those people have, if any, about who they do or do not want to assemble with, however, those people do not necessarily need to have any Public Notice and do not necessarily need to adhere to any of their Public Notices in any particular situation involving any particular person.

E

The Purpose of this Section is to make it generally easier for members of the Public, to locate and assemble with other groups of people who have similar likes and dislikes as themselves, for the purposes of doing legal activities, such as, seeking employment, or seeking a place to rent.

Section 3 of 3. Interpretation of this Law by US Voters.

If any part of this Law needs Interpretation by a Federal Court in the United States, after any part of this Law is enacted to be an Amendment to the US Constitution, then such an Interpretation shall be asked to be done by the Voters of the United States, and shall not be done by any Federal Court in the United States.

PART B. DUTIES OF CONGRESSPERSONS OF THIS STATE; INTERPRETATION OF THIS LAW; PAYING THE PROPONENT OF THIS LAW.

Section 1 of 3. Duties of Congresspersons.

(Put Chapter 3 here
- the Control Your Congress Clause)

Section 2 of 3. Amending and Interpreting this State Law.

(Put Chapter 4 here - the Interpretation Clause)

Section 3 of 3. Paying the Bill.

(Put Chapter 5 here
- the Reimbursement Clause)

* * * *

E

F

Example Petition:

Judicial Department
Improvement Act

F

State and Federal Law

(**free to copy and modify**)

Short Titles used within this Act:

* A. Creation of the Judicial Department
   Improvement Act

* B. Questions Of Law to be interpreted by
   Legislature

* C. Right to have Civil and Criminal Court
   Cases dismissed by Jury

* D. State Legislature to decide when Judges
   can be sued

F

GENERAL PREAMBLE TO THIS ACT.

This Law Protects you from Judges, many of whom
may be Unfair, Corrupt, or have their own Agenda.

Generally speaking, Judges often develop feelings of dislike towards a Lawyer in a Court Case, or towards a Party in the Court Case, as the Court Case progresses towards a Court Trial, resulting in premature dismissals by those Judges that often result in time consuming Court Appeals, and Additional Court Costs and Legal fees.

This Law Creates Safeguards to protect you against Judges who prematurely dismiss Court Cases, Incorrectly Interpret Laws; this Law also forces the Legislators to determine when Judges can be sued in a Civil Court after a Judge illegally Orders something to be done.

Lawyers will agree, this Law will be immensely valuable in protecting you in Court.

We the People thank GOD for this Law.

PART A. CREATION OF THE JUDICIAL DEPARTMENT IMPROVEMENT ACT.

Section 1 of 2. Creation of Act; Title of Act.

This Law Creates an Judicial Department Improvement Act that may be Cited as the Judicial Department Improvement Act.

PART B. QUESTIONS OF LAW TO BE INTERPRETED BY LEGISLATURE.

Section 1 of 2. Questions of Law arising in Court, or in a Government Agency.

All Judges in the jurisdiction of this State, while presiding over a Court Hearing, shall be allowed to Answer Questions of Law, when allowed by Law, however, if any Party in the Court Case has a Right to Appeal the Interpretation, or in the event the Interpretation is Done by the Highest Appellate Court, and the Party is not satisfied with the Interpretation done by the Judge or Judges, then the Party may ask that the appropriate Government Legislature, be called for the purposes of Interpreting the Question of Law, and any subsequent Interpretation done by the Legislature will allow the Court Case to continue for all intents and purposes.

At the time that an Interpretation is sought to be done by the appropriate Government Legislature, all the various Interpretations sought by the Judge or Judges, and the Parties to the Court Case, shall be given to the Legislature.

F

After the appropriate Government Legislature does its Interpretation of the Question of Law, and thereby allows the Court Case to Continue for all intents and purposes, the Legislature shall determine if a Formal Amendment of the Law can only be done by the appropriate Voters who enacted the Law, and if so, then the Question of Law, along with the various Interpretations sought by the Judge and the Parties to the Court Case, along with the Interpretation done by the appropriate Legislature for any Court Case, along with any other Interpretation that any member of the Legislature wants to offer to the Voters, shall all be given to the appropriate Voters, at the Normal Designated Time that such Laws are Voted for, unless another Time is Set by the appropriate Legislature Prior to the Normal Designated Time for the Voters to Vote for the Interpretations.

If a Formal Amendment can be done by the Legislature without the Voters Approval, then the Legislature shall amend the Law, so as to Include their Interpretation into the Law.

Nothing in this Section prevents the Same Law to be presented a Second Time to the appropriate Government Legislature, for another Interpretation, and when presented a Second Time, the Judge or Judges presiding in the Court Hearing are not allowed to decide the Validity of any New Question of Law pertaining to the Same Law, and only the Legislature may determine how the Legislature will preliminarily review the Same Law being presented a Second Time for the purposes of deciding whether to Interpret the Law or not a Second Time.

F

For the purposes of this Part, any Government Agency may present a Question of Law directly to the appropriate Legislature for an Interpretation, consistent with this Part as if the Question of Law originated in a Court, and then the Legislature shall Interpret the Law, consistent with this Section as if the Question of Law originated in a Court, and the Government Agency can act on the Interpretation done by the Legislature, or if applicable, may decide to wait for an Interpretation to be done by the Voters.

Whenever a Question of Law is given to the Voters, each and every Interpretation included that was done by any Government Employee, shall be Tagged with the Name and Office Address of the Government Employee who had that particular Interpretation or Interpretations, so as to allow the Public to have an opinion about that particular Government Employee.

For the purposes of this Law:

* appropriate Government Legislature means the State Legislature for State Laws, and a Local Government Legislature for Local Laws;

* appropriate Voters means the State Voters for State Laws, and the Local Voters for Local Laws.

Section 2 of 2. Time to Answer Questions of Law.

After a Question of Law is presented to the Appropriate Government Legislature, pursuant to this Law, along with the Interpretation sought by the Judge or Judges, and each Party to the Court Case, the Legislature shall answer the Question of Law within 30 days, unless the State Legislature extends the time for a particular Interpretation, and if desired, the Legislature may limit their time used to Interpret the Law, to Vote from the Interpretations that were offered by the Judge or Judges, and Parties to the Court Case, for the purposes of allowing the Court Case to Continue for all intents and purposes.

F

PART C. RIGHT TO HAVE CIVIL AND CRIMINAL COURT CASES DISMISSED BY JURY.

Section 1 of 2. Dismissal of Court Cases.

All Judges presiding over a Court Case in the jurisdiction of this State, shall be allowed to Dismiss a Court Case if allowed by Law, however, if any Party in the Court Case has a Right to Appeal the Dismissal, and is not satisfied with the Dismissal by the Judge, then the Party may ask that a Jury be called for the purposes of deciding if the Court Case should be Dismissed, instead of Appealing the Dismissal as otherwise allowed by Law.

During any Appeal of a Dismissal pursuant to this Law, if the Jury or the Appellate Court Court does not Uphold the Dismissal of the Judge, then the Jury or Appellate Court shall also decide if the Court Case should be transferred to another Judge who will then preside over the Case, at least until the next Dismissal Hearing pursuant to this Law.

Section 2 of 2. Duties of State Legislature.

The State Legislature shall enact State Laws that regulate:

* how a Jury shall be called to dismiss a Court Case, pursuant to this Law, and how many Jury Members shall be called;

* if and when dismissals decided by a Jury can be appealed to an Appellate Court or elsewhere;

* what Jury Fees will be charged to any particular Party in the Court Case, if any are charged, and when those Fees can be waived, such as for persons with insufficient funds.

F

PART D. PRIVATE ATTORNEYS CAN PROSECUTE CRIMINAL CASES; CRIMINAL AND CIVIL CASES TO BE JOINED.

Section 1 of 2. Private Attorneys can prosecute Criminal Cases.

Any Private Attorney who is admitted to the State Bar for Attorneys in this State, is allowed to initiate and prosecute any type of criminal case that the State and Local Government Prosecuting Attorneys in this State are allowed to initiate and prosecute; after a Private Attorney initiates a criminal case, any Government Prosecuting Attorney who would have had jurisdiction to initiate the prosecution, is allowed to join the prosecution.

Section 2 of 2. Criminal Cases and Civil Cases to be joined into one Case.

Any cause that can give rise to both a criminal case and a civil case, shall be joined into one case;

a plaintiff or defendant in any joined case, will maintain any right to public defender for the prosecution or the defense;

during sentencing, the jury or judge in any joined case shall determine both the criminal and civil punishments;

any party in any joined case, may employ a Private Attorney admitted to the State Bar to participate in the joined case.

PART E. STATE LEGISLATURE TO DECIDE WHEN JUDGES CAN BE SUED.

Section 1 of 2. Legislature to Review all Laws and Cases about Judges being sued in the United States.

F

The State Legislature shall review:

* all the State Laws in the United States that pertain to both Judicial Immunity and when Judges Can be sued;

* all the State and Federal Court Opinions, in the United States, made by Judges, pertaining to when a Judge was sued, including the very first Court Opinions in the United States that first established the use of Judicial Immunity in the United States.

Section 2 of 2. State Legislature to Enacts Laws about when Judges can be sued.

After reviewing all the facts and opinions pursuant to Section 1 of this Law, the State Legislature shall enact one or more State Laws that describe when a Judge can be sued in a State Civil Court in this State by a member of the public.

PART F. INTERPRETATION OF THIS LAW; TIME FOR STATE LEGISLATURE TO ENACT LAWS PURSUANT TO THIS LAW; DUTIES OF CONGRESSPERSONS OF THIS STATE.

Section 1 of 5. Amending and Interpreting this State Law; Time to Enact Laws pursuant to this State Law.

(Put Chapter 4 here - the Interpretation Clause)
{ Also include the following... }

After this Law is enacted, and before the next General Election, the State Legislature shall enact all the required Laws as described in Part C and D of this Law.

Section 2 of 5. Duties of Congresspersons of this State, pertaining to Part B and Part C of this Law.

Each Congressperson elected to represent this State in the United States Congress, shall during each session of the US Congress, if they are present during said session, petition the other members of the US Congress who are present during the session, to enact one or more US Laws that have the same effect as Part B, C, and D of this Law when applied to Federal Courts and Federal Court Cases.

F

Section 3 of 5. Duties of Congresspersons of this State, pertaining to Part D of this Law.

Each person elected by the citizens of this State, who are elected to serve this State in the Congress of the United States of America, whether as a Senator or a Representative, shall immediately work together during their terms of office, and propose or maintain similar Bills, in both houses of Congress, calling for a Congressional Committee that must:

* collect all the Laws and Court Opinions as described in this Law pertaining to a Judge being sued within the United States borders;

* review all of those Laws and Court Opinions collected;

* propose a Bill that describes in detail when and how a Federal Judge can be sued, and can not be sued, by a member of the public;

* propose a Bill that describes how the United States Congress shall periodically review the effects of the Federal Laws that are enacted by the United States Congress pertaining to when a Federal Judge can be sued, and can not be sued, by a member of the public.

(Put the remainder of Chapter 3 here
- the Control Your Congress Clause)

Section 4 of 5. General Duties of Congresspersons of this State, pertaining to Petitioning the US Congress pursuant to this Part.

The Congresspersons of this State, must Petition the other members of the US Congress, pertaining to the items described in this Part, at each session of the United States Congress, until the described US Laws are enacted, however, pertaining to Judges being sued, if the US Congressional Committee is formed pursuant to Section 4 in this Part, then the Repetitious Petition pertaining to Judges being sued may be limited to asking the US Congress for a progress report about the enactment of the US Laws pertaining to Judges being sued.

F

After any US Laws are enacted pursuant to this Law, the Congresspersons of this State must get a Majority Vote from the Voters of this State, before the Congresspersons of this State can Vote for any subsequent US Laws that have the effect of contradicting Parts B, C, or E of this Law.

Section 5 of 5. Paying the Bill.

(Put Chapter 5 here
- the Reimbursement Clause)

*　*　*　*

G

Example Petition:

State Transportation Improvement Act

State Law

G

(free to copy and modify)

Short Titles used within this Act:

* A. Creation of the State Transportation
   Improvement Act

* B. Vehicle Liability Insurance paid with
   Gas Tax

* C. Vehicle Registration Fees paid with
   Gas Tax

G

Preamble of the Law.

This is a State Law, that is enacted by the Voters, and therefore, the State Legislature is allowed to propose amendments to the Voters if needed after this Law is Enacted.

This Law allows you to pay your Vehicle Liability Insurance, and Vehicle Registration Fees, by the mile, using a Gas Tax.

If you drive more, you pay more.

If you drive less, you pay less.

This Law GUARANTEES that all victims of Motor Vehicle Accidents will get reimbursed for their Injuries and Damages, because this Law GUARANTEES that all Vehicles in this State are covered by Liability Insurance;

It should be noted that Liability Insurance only reimburses the victims that do not cause the Motor Vehicle Accident.

This Law will substantially reduce your Current Vehicle Liability Insurance Payments, because the State is not a Private Insurance Company getting a profit from the Insurance Payments;

When enacted, the Gas Tax should be substantially less than what you are paying now to Private Insurance Companies.

Another benefit this Law provides, is that you can park your car, truck, or motorcycle, for extended periods of time, without having to pay Vehicle Registration Fees and Liability Insurance, just so you can drive your Vehicle once in awhile throughout the year.

Note: This Law does not provide Extended Insurance Coverage, and Extended Coverage will need to be sought from Private Insurance Companies.

As a result of this Law paying all your Vehicle Registration Fees using a Gas Tax:

 * you will not need to pay any Registration Fees, Late Fees, Penalty Fees, or Non-Operational Fees to operate your Motor Vehicle.

* the State will not need to spend hundreds of thousands of dollars every year for Administrative Fees just to process those Vehicle Registration Payments.

G

* more Jobs and Revenue may be temporarily created in this State, until more States adopt this Law, because this Law encourages owners of Commercial Vehicles used in Interstate Commerce, who can Register their Vehicles in any State, to register their Vehicle or Fleet of Vehicles in this State, instead of another State,and will thereby increase some Jobs and Revenues in this State;

the Increased Revenues would include Property Sales and Property Rentals used by those persons, Sales of Vehicle Products sold to those persons, and monies spent in-State by their employees.

Once again, this is a State Law that is enacted by the Voters, and therefore, the State Legislature is allowed to propose necessary amendments to the Voters if needed.

We the People thank GOD for this Law.

PART A. CREATION OF THE STATE TRANSPORTATION IMPROVEMENT ACT.

Section 1 of 1. Creation of Act;

Title of Act.

This Law Creates a Transportation Improvement Act that may be Cited as the State Transportation Improvement Act.

PART B. STATE LIABILITY INSURANCE PAID WITH GAS TAX.

Section 1 of 3. Liability Insurance paid with Gas Tax.

A Gas Tax is hereby enacted, to be regulated by the State Legislature, and the Collected Gas Tax shall be put into a Vehicle Liability Insurance Fund.

All State Liability Insurance for Motor Vehicles,required by the State, will be covered by the Vehicle Liability Insurance Fund.

G

This Law does not prevent the State Legislature to enact State Laws pertaining to Suspending Driver Licenses or Imposing other Punishments towards persons convicted of Reckless Driving.

Section 2 of 3. This Law to be fully effective and in use before next General Election.

A 1% Gas Tax is to take effect at the time this Law is Enacted, to begin the Vehicle Liability Insurance Fund.

Before the next General Election, the State Legislature shall enact State Laws that:

* regulate the amount of Gas Tax to charge in any given year, to maintain the Vehicle Liability Insurance Fund.

* regulate how Court Cases and Investigations involving Motor Vehicle Accidents shall be conducted, so as to prevent Fraud and to insure that the appropriate Injured persons are paid appropriate amounts of money from the Vehicle Liability Insurance Fund;

such State Laws will also regulate how the State will participate in Out-of-State Court Cases and Investigations when Residents of this State drive out of the State.

Section 3 of 3. Residents Fully Covered when Law Enacted.

One month from the time this Law is Enacted, all Residents of this State, while driving in or out of this State, and all other Non-Residents while driving in this State, will all be fully covered by the minimum Vehicle Liability Insurance required in this State, to be paid for using the Vehicle Liability Insurance Fund, however, Non-Residents driving in this State who have Liability Insurance paid for by another Insurance Party, shall be covered by the Liability Insurance of the other Party, and will not be covered by the Liability Insurance of this State, and those Non-Residents also will not be covered by the Liability Insurance of this State if that other Insurance Party includes in their Insurance Policy an Exclusion from providing Liability Coverage for persons driving in States that pay for Liability Insurance.

G

All of the Gas Tax collected by the State Legislature for any given year to fund the Vehicle Liability Insurance Fund, shall be estimated to be an amount that is approximately twice the amount needed to cover Liability Insurance and the other costs associated with Liability Insurance for the next year, such as Investigations and Litigation, however, the State Legislature may attempt to maintain a different amount.

If the Vehicle Liability Insurance Fund is depleted to $0 at any given time, then the State shall resume any Obligation to pay any Injured Persons Entitled to Funds from the Vehicle Liability Insurance Fund, without Interest, at the time any Gas Tax replenishes the Vehicle Liability Insurance Fund.

PART C. VEHICLE REGISTRATION FEES PAID WITH GAS TAX.

Section 1 of 3. Vehicle Registration Fees paid with Gas Tax.

A Gas Tax is hereby enacted, to be regulated by the State Legislature, and the Collected Gas Tax shall be put into a Vehicle Registration Fund.

All Vehicle Registration Fees collected by this State, from Residents of this State, and Non-Residents, will be collected from the Vehicle Registration Fund;

G

however, if such Vehicles are owned or leased by Non-Residents and are involved in Interstate Commercial Use, then those Non-Residents must Rent, Lease, or own,at the minimum, one permanent Address in this State, of a sufficient size that would accommodate all the Vehicles that the Non-Resident wants to Register in this State, if the Non-Resident were to parked all of those Vehicles at the same time at the permanent Address or Addresses;

if the Non-Resident does not have such an Address or Addresses, then one standard Vehicle Registration Fee, for any type of vehicle, may be charged to those Non-Residents for each of their Commercial Vehicles that can not be accommodated by the Address or Addresses.

This Law pays for certain Fees, but this Law does not change any State Laws pertaining to:

* getting a Vehicle Registered, such as when the Title of Ownership Changes, or the Residence Address Changes.

* getting required Vehicle Inspections;

all the required Vehicle Inspections shall be paid using the Vehicle Registration Fund, however, one standard Vehicle Inspection Fee may be charged for each Vehicle Inspection that is not Mandatory.

* getting required Smog Tests;

and the State Legislature can enact State Laws that require people to Carry a Smog Certificate showing that a Vehicle Passes a Smog Test, and to fine people who drive their vehicles without having a Smog Certificate in their Vehicle, or who drive their vehicles without passing a required Smog Test;

176

all the required Smog Tests and Re-Tests, shall be paid using the Vehicle Registration Fund, however, one standard Smog Test Fee may be charged for each Smog Test that is not Mandatory.

Section 2 of 3. This Law to be fully effective and in use at the Time this Law Enacted.

A 1% Gas Tax is to take effect at the time this Law is Enacted, to begin the Vehicle Registration Fund.

Before the next General Election, the State Legislature shall enact State Laws that:

G

* regulate the amount of Gas Tax to charge in any given year, to maintain the Vehicle Registration Fund;

* regulate how Non-Residents shall provide Proof of Address for any of their Vehicles involved in Interstate Commercial Use, and until that time, such Non-Residents may provide Proof of Address in the form of an Affidavit under Penalty of Perjury.

Section 3 of 3. Required Vehicle Registration Fees Fully Paid when Law Enacted.

One month from the time this Law is Enacted, all Vehicles Registration Fees in this State will be paid by the Vehicle Registration Fund, according to the terms of this Part.

All of the Gas Tax Laws the State Legislature enacts for any given year to fund the Vehicle Registration Fund, shall try to estimate and maintain an amount of money in the Vehicle Registration Fund, that is approximately twice the amount needed to cover Vehicle Registration Fees, however, the State Legislature may attempt to maintain a greater amount.

If the Vehicle Registration Funds are depleted at any given time, then required Vehicle Registrations will be done without Funds, or postponed, until the Gas Tax replenishes the Vehicle Registration Fund, unless the State Legislature can borrow the moneys, interest free, from another source.

PART D. CONFORMITY TO OTHER LAWS; INTERPRETATIONS; AMENDMENTS; PAYING THE PROPONENT OF THIS LAW.

Section 1 of 3. Conformity to Other Laws.

If necessary to enable the State Legislature to comply with all Provisions of this Law, the State Legislature shall Propose to the Voters the necessary amendments to the State Constitution that are needed;

And if necessary to enable the State Legislature to comply with all Provisions of this Law, the State Legislature shall also amend the necessary State Laws directly themselves, or Propose to the Voters the necessary amendments to State Laws if amendments to those State Laws are required by Law to be proposed to the Voters rather than directly amended by the State Legislature;

G

And if any amendments are necessary, or if the State Legislature otherwise needs to Conform to the Legal Requirements of any State Constitutional Law, or State Law, before this Law can become Fully Effective so as to enable the two Funds to be fully accessible by the State Government for the intents and purposes of this Law:

the State Legislature shall attempt,if necessary, to borrow the Moneys needed to fund the two Funds from other sources, if such Moneys can be borrowed interest free;

and if the Moneys can not be borrowed interest free, then any debts owed by the State Government to various persons according to and pursuant to this Law, shall be temporarily accrued by the State Government, and then paid Interest Free, as the two Funds are funded and become fully accessible by the State Government;

And more specifically, the State Legislature may need to propose an Amendment to [Article19 of the State Constitutional Law, or such and such State Constitutional Law], that was previously proposed and approved by the Voters, that regulates how the State Government spends Gas Taxes, however, unless the issue is taken to Court about the interpretation of [Article 19], the State Legislature is hereby authorized to interpret [Article 19] as being a Law that only tells the State Government what to do, pertaining to the State Government enacting a Gas Tax, and shall not be interpreted as a Law that tells the Voters what to do, pertaining to the Voters of this State trying to Impose a Gas Tax on themselves.

Section 2 of 3. Amending and Interpreting this State Law.

(Put Chapter 4 here - the Interpretation Clause)

Section 3 of 3. Paying the Bill.

(Put Chapter 5 here - the Reimbursement Clause)

* * * *

G

H

Example Petition:

Graffiti Law

H

State Law

(free to copy and modify)

Preamble of the Law.

Certain persons have a tendency of illegally putting graffiti onto public and private property, including, but not limited to, trucks, box vans, trailers, recreational vehicles, buildings, traffic control signs, sign posts, fences, walls, bridges, trees, plants, sidewalks, etc.

Many people who do graffiti, tend to consistently put graffiti onto property, and it can be presumed that those persons will do a Felonies worth of damage.

H

Many people who have had graffiti on their Vehicle or other Property can recall how upset they were.

Graffiti is costing people hundreds of thousands of dollars each year, and is not pleasant to look at.

The Voters may not be aware of it, but many of those people who are putting graffiti onto items, are driving around town in their personal vehicles as they do their graffiti.

This Law, protects YOUR PROPERTY, pays for the Damage Done, pays for a Reward, and after a couple Arrests pursuant to this Law, this Law will be a Strong Deterrent to persons who habitually put Graffiti onto your property for their own amusement.

We the People thank GOD for this Law.

PART A. GRAFFITI LAW.

Section 1 of 4. Graffiti is a Felony.

The State Legislature, shall determine what category of Felonies to charge persons who are convicted of putting Graffiti onto any Public or Private property within this State.

For the purposes of this Law, Graffiti shall include, but not be limited to, property defaced with Spray Paint, Pen Marker, Scratches, and Flame producing lighters.

The State Legislature, may categorize their felonies, and allow for early parole after imprisonment for those convicted persons who forfeited one ore more vehicles pursuant this Law, and the State Legislature may also determine eligibility for parole based on the value of those vehicles forfeited, such as, no parole may be granted until after 1 year of imprisonment if an accused person forfeited one or more vehicles that was sold for a total $200 or less, and such as, early parole may be granted after 2 months if an accused person forfeited one or more vehicles that was sold for a total of $20,000 or more.

H

The people of this State, demand that all persons who put graffiti onto items not belonging to them, and accomplices to those persons, shall be arrested and accused of disobeying this Graffiti Law.

Section 2 of 4. Determining Guilt at scene of crime.

At the crime scene, Law Enforcement shall attempt to determine who owns the property with graffiti on it, and if the accused persons had permission to put graffiti onto the property.

If Law Enforcement determines that an arrested person has a most favorable probability of conviction, then Law Enforcement shall seize and search all the vehicles owned by the arrested person, be it one or more vehicles, and where ever those vehicles may be located.

If Law Enforcement determines that an arrested person does not have a favorable probability of conviction, then Law Enforcement may search but not seize all the vehicles owned by the arrested person.

Also based on a determination of a favorable probability of conviction of an arrested person, Law Enforcement has a right to Search the verifiable Resident Address or Addresses on record of an arrested person, even if the arrested person is a minor, and during such search, Law Enforcement may search for any type of illegal items anywhere at the Residence to the extent allowed by the State Legislature and to the extent desired by the Law Enforcement Officers.

Section 3 of 4. Arrested person forfeit their vehicles upon conviction; residential searches allowed if not already done.

H

If the accused are later Convicted for their Crimes, Law Enforcement shall seize and search all the vehicles owned by the accused, be it one or more vehicles, where ever those vehicles may be located, if Law Enforcement has not already done so pursuant to Section 1 of this Law.

Also, after conviction, Law Enforcement, have aright to Search the Resident Addresses of the person arrested, within 1 month of conviction, if Law Enforcement has not already done so pursuant to Section 1 of this Law, even if the arrested person is a minor, and during such searches, Law Enforcement shall search for illegal items to the extent allowed by Law and to the extent desired by the Law Enforcement Officers.

Upon conviction, the convicted persons shall forfeit all the vehicles that were seized pursuant to this Law.

Section 4 of 4. Sale of confiscated vehicles.

All Vehicles confiscated pursuant to this Law shall be sold according to Law.

The greater of $200 or 25% of the sale of those confiscated vehicles shall be given as a reward to the person or persons who reported the graffiti, be it a private citizen or a police officer.

After the reward is given or attempted, 25% of the remaining money of the sale of those confiscated vehicles, if any amount remaining above the $200 reward, shall be given to the owners who had the graffiti put onto their property, even if they already collected the $200 reward for reporting the crime;

if more than one owner is involved, then the Jury, or the Judge if no Jury is used, shall divvy up the25% amongst the owners according to evidence presented to the Court;

additional evidence may be presented by the owners involved, and all the owners on record, as reported by Law Enforcement, shall be notified by the Clerks of the Court about when the owners can testify in Court about how much damage was done to their property, and how much of the Reward they are Entitled to.

H

The State Legislature shall enact Laws about how to use, or give as Reward, the remaining 50%, and until such time, 10% shall be given to the police officer who does the arrests, or equally shared by the police officers who do the arrests, and 10% shall be given to the victims of the Graffiti using the methods described above, and 10% shall be given to the persons who reported the Graffiti as the Graffiti was happening, and 20% shall be put into the Local General Fund for Graffiti Removal.

PART B. CONFORMITY TO OTHER LAWS; INTERPRETATIONS; AMENDMENTS; PAYING THE PROPONENT OF THIS LAW.

Section 1 of 2. Amending and Interpreting this State Law.

(Put Chapter 4 here - the Interpretation Clause)

Section 2 of 2. Paying the Bill.

(Put Chapter 5 here - the Reimbursement Clause)

* * * *

I

Example Petition:

The People's Law about Prisons

I

State and Federal Law

(free to copy and modify)

Preamble of the Law.

This Law upholds the Innocent-Until-Proven-Guilty doctrine, and forces Law Enforcement to separate arrested adults and children, from Convicted Persons, while those arrested adults and children are waiting for Trial.

Many people have seen prison movies of Convicted Persons locked up together, and what happens as the result.

Often a person is locked up with other convicted persons, who may or may not have done a more serious crime.

When locked up together, Convicted persons are allowed to abuse each other, manipulative each other, form gangs, socialize, tell each other about their crimes, and how to do them better when they get out of jail, etc.

This Law says that Convicted persons, shall not be allowed see, visit, or otherwise communicate with each other, as much as practical, for the entire duration of their imprisonment.

We the People thank GOD for this Law.

Section 1 of 5. Persons waiting for Trial to be separated from convicted persons.

All arrested persons in this State, shall be separated from, and not allowed to have contact with, Convicted Persons, until after they are Convicted.

This Section takes effect within 7 days after this Law is Approved by the Voters, if not sooner, to give Notice to the wardens of the Prisons and Jails in this State that this Law is in effect.

Section 2 of 5. Convicted Persons to be Separated from each other as much as practical.

All persons imprisoned in this State, shall as much a practical, be separated from all contact with each other, and in situations when not practical, those imprisoned persons must at a minimum be separated from all contact with each other within the Prison Facility according to their Race, including in the Prison Kitchens and elsewhere in the Prison facility.

All New Prison Facilities in this State, shall as much as practical, be built and maintained so as to conform to this Law.

The Prison Facilities used by this State have 1 year to comply with this Section after this Law is Approved by the Voters.

For the purposes of this Law, the term Prison Facility also includes Jail Facility, and also includes any Out-of-State Prison or Jail Facility, if any, that may be used by this State to house prisoners of this State.

Section 3 of 5. Duties of State's Congresspersons.

Each person elected by the citizens of this State, who are elected to serve this State in the Congress of the United States of America, whether as a Senator or a Representative, shall immediately work together during their terms of office, and propose or maintain similar Bills, in both houses of Congress, calling for a Federal Law containing Text similar to Section 1 and Section 2 of this State Law.

(Put the remainder of Chapter 3 here - the Control Your Congress Clause)

Section 4 of 5. Amending and Interpreting this State Law.

(Put Chapter 4 here - the Interpretation Clause)

Section 5 of 5. Paying the Bill.

(Put Chapter 5 here- the Reimbursement Clause)

* * * *

J

Example Petition:

US Government not allowed to give money to Foreigners

J

US Constitutional Law

(free to copy and modify)

Preamble of the Law.

This Law prevents the US Congress from giving Money to Foreigners, without the explicit approval of the US Voters in any particular situation.

This Law prevents the US Executive Department from giving Money to anyone, without the explicit approval of the US Congress in any particular situation.

This Law prevents the US Government from Secretly giving billions of dollars of Tax Money to Foreigners, their own Personal Bank Accounts, or Others, without the Approval of the US Congress.

J

This Law should help to improve Accountability of the US Executive Department, and reduce the US Deficit.

We the People thank GOD for this Law.

PART A. US GOVERNMENT SPENDING.

Section 1 of 5. US Executive Department needs Congressional approval for money.

The US Executive Department can not give Money to anyone not employed in the US Executive Department, without the explicit approval of the US Congress pursuant to a majority vote of the US Congress.

Section 2 of 5. US Executive Department needs Congressional approval for money.

The US Executive Department can not give Money to anyone not employed in the US Executive Department, without the explicit approval of the US Congress pursuant to a majority vote of the US Congress.

Section 3 of 5. US Congress to audit US Executive Department.

The US Congress shall appoint a committee composed of independent investigators answerable to the US Congress;

each investigator shall be responsible to thoroughly investigate and audit how the US Executive Department spends any money Given to the US Executive Department by the US Congress.

Section 4 of 5. Duties of the US Congress.

The US Congress shall enact US Laws to govern both the US Congress and the US Executive Department in obeying this this Law;

the US Congress shall also enact uniform US Laws withing ___2___ years of the enactment of this US Constitutional Amendment, for the sole purpose of governing how each Department of the US Government will provide records to any Certified Public Accountant who is a resident of the US for the sole purpose of allowing the private Certified Accountants to a private audit of any Department of the US Government, for the sole purpose of showing the Certified Public Accountants how 100% of the US funds are being spent by the US Government;

J

the US Congress shall specify that any disobedience of the US Congress in providing the records specified by the US Congress shall be a felony punishable by not less than ___4___ years in the Federal Penitentiary.

Section 5 of 5. Interpretation of this Law by the US Congress.

If any part of this Law needs Interpretation by a Federal Court in the United States, or other Federal Government Agency of the United States, after any part of this Law is enacted to be an Amendment to the US Constitution, then such an Interpretation shall be done by a Federal Court;

the Federal Court shall then ask the US Congress for their Interpretation;

the US Congress shall then ask the US Voters to approve of one, all, or none of the Interpretations provided to the US Voters by the US Congress;

the Voters of any Particular state may also vote by majority vote that other interpretations be provided to the US Voters at the same time that the US Congress provides Interpretations to the US Voters for approval or disapproval;

all Interpretations approved by the US Voters shall be included into and amend the Amendment to the US Constitution.

PART B. DUTIES OF CONGRESSPERSONS OF THIS STATE; INTERPRETATION OF THIS STATE LAW; AMENDMENTS; PAYING THE PROPONENT OF THIS LAW.

Section 1 of 3. Duties of Congresspersons of this State.

Each person elected by the citizens of this State, who are elected to serve this State in the Congress of the United States of America, whether as a Senator or a Representative, shall immediately work together during their terms of office, and propose or maintain similar Bills, in both houses of Congress, calling for an Amendment to the United States Constitution that includes all the text included in Part A of this Law; (put the remainder of Chapter 3 here - the Control Your Congress Clause);

J

Whenever the State Legislature is asked to Vote for the Constitutional Amendment, as described in this Section, then the State Legislature shall approve of the Amendment unless the Amendment is different than what is proposed in this Law, and in that situation, then the State Legislature shall give the Amendment to the Voters of this State for their Approval.

Section 2 of 3. Amending and Interpreting this State Law.

(Put Chapter 4 here - the Interpretation Clause)

Section 3 of 3. Paying the Bill.

(Put Chapter 5 here - the Reimbursement Clause)

* * * *

K

Example Petition:

The People's Law about Food Labels

State Law

K

(free to copy and modify)

Preamble of the Law.

This Law forces Food Ingredient Labels to include details about the food you eat, such as what are in the spices, natural flavors, artificial flavors, and food colorings, gmo's, et cetera.

We the People thank GOD for this Law.

Section 1 of 4. Vague words must be replaced with specific words.

All Ingredient Food Labels on Foods Sold In this State, must list in detail the ingredients in the food.

K

For example:

* "Spice" shall be replaced with the particular name of the Spice used, such as "Black Pepper", or "Oregano".

* "Natural Flavor" shall be replaced with the specific name of the Natural Flavor used, such as "Natural Flavor from Oranges", or "Oranges".

* "Artificial Flavor" shall be replaced with the specific name of the Artificial Flavor that is being used.

* "Artificial Color" shall be replaced with what the coloring is made of, such as "Artificial Color from ...".

* "Natural Color" shall be replaced with what the coloring is made of, such as "Natural Color from ...".

* all foods that are gmo's shall be labeled as gmo food.

Section 2 of 4. Time to comply with this Law.

Pursuant to this Law, the Manufacturers and Sellers of Food shall comply with this Law, according to this Law, before the next General Election.

Section 3 of 4. Amending and Interpreting this State Law.

(Put Chapter 4 here - the Interpretation Clause)

Section 4 of 4. Paying the Bill.

(Put Chapter 5 here - the Reimbursement Clause)

* * * *

K

L

Example Petition:

A Fresh Approach
to
Legalizing Marijuana

L

State Law

ANOTHER GOOD DAY WITH GOD

Preamble of the Law.

Whereas God the creator of the Universe made the plant called marijuana, and whereas the use of marijuana throughout history has shown that marijuana is safe for human consumption, and that the current medical view of marijuana by many doctors of medicine is that marijuana is safe for human consumption, and whereas the use of marijuana throughout history has shown that marijuana is also safe for animal consumption because wild animals such as deer commonly consume marijuana safely as a part of their normal diet, and whereas many Countries, such as Holland, and the Netherlands, and many other Countries, allow the use of marijuana for human consumption without any major issues, else it would be prohibited there, and whereas Marijuana would be safer regulated than not regulated, similar to the Issues of Alcohol before and after the Prohibition Era, and whereas the first Illegalization of marijuana in the United States, was based on False Propaganda against Marijuana, possibly using Bribes, and possibly because of the Competition of Wood versus

L

Marijuana in the Manufacture of Paper, this State Law is hereby enacted by the Voters of this State.

Once Approved by the Voters, this Law waits __2__ years before Voiding all the State Laws that prohibit General Marijuana Use in this State, and thereby gives the Local Voters, within their Respective County and City Jurisdictions, an opportunity to prohibit any aspect of Marijuana Use within their County or City Jurisdictions before Voiding the State Laws that prohibit General Marijuana Use in this State.

Consumers of marijuana are also notified, in this Preamble, that marijuana is edible, and need not be inhaled, and can be eaten alone as a food item, or mixed with other foods, such as sauces, brownies, and sprinkled onto foods such as salads.

Consumers of marijuana are also notified, in this Preamble, that marijuana is easy to grow, and as such, the price for a pound of marijuana if being bought or sold, could be compared to the price of a pound of carrots, or a pound lettuce, or a pound of potatoes, et cetera.

This State Law also calls for the repeal of the Federal Marijuana Laws passed by the US Congress, by forcing the Congresspersons of this State to petition the US Congress to give the Right to Prohibit Marijuana to the States, thereby putting the Regulation into the Jurisdiction of the States, and during that time, this State Law prepares this State for that repeal.

It may be important to many people to point out the fact that this State Law does not amend or abolish any Internal Policy ALREADY IN USE by any State or Local Governmental Agency and Private Business in this State that prohibits marijuana use by their employees, or by people on the property they manage, and therefore, * this Law SUPPORTS any Internal Policy that prohibits School Bus Drivers from using marijuana;

* this Law SUPPORTS other Internal Policies of that prohibits any other Company Drivers from using marijuana;

* this Law ALLOWS Government Agency's and Private Business's to collect urine samples, and to obtain results of urine samples, for any applicant, for any Job, according to Internal Policy, and then refuse or restrict employment to that person if marijuana is found;

* this Law ALLOWS Insurance Companies to collect urine samples, and to obtain results of urine samples, according to their Internal Policies, and then raise their Insurance Rates based on the results of those urine samples, if they want to;

* this Law DOES NOT "Legalize" Marijuana in any shape or form;

* this Law DOES NOT prevent any Federal Agency from enforcing a Congressional Federal Marijuana Law within this State;

* this Law ALLOWS Local Counties, Cities, Towns, and Communities, by majority vote of the voters, to Prohibit Marijuana Use within their jurisdictions;

* this Law ALLOWS the State Legislature to enact State Laws that prohibit Marijuana Use by State employees of the State Government.

This State Law simply prevents the State Legislature itself, from enacting Marijuana Laws that prohibit the Public from using Marijuana, and passes that choice to prohibit ANY form of Marijuana Use, to the voters of the Local Counties, Cities, Towns, Communities, and other Entities.

After this Law is enacted, the Proponent of this Law estimates that about the same amount of adults will be using Marijuana in this State pursuant to this State Law as were using Marijuana before this State Law, such as a few Senior Citizens, Retired Persons, Vacationers, Medical Users, and a few others not subject to a Local Law, Internal Policy, and Urine Samples, but the main difference is that it will not be Illegal or Prosecuted under State Law, and perhaps Federal Law after the Federal Marijuana Laws are repealed.

This State Law also Creates an Agency of Marijuana Statistics in this State, that will have Marijuana Statistics and other Marijuana Information available to the Public.

It should also be noted, that this is a State Law, and not an Amendment to the State Constitution, **L** and therefore, the Voters will be able to propose later Amendments to this Law with less signatures if the voters want an Amendment.

We the People thank GOD for this Law.

Section 1 of 17. Congressperson of this State must Petition Congress to Repeal Marijuana Laws.

Each person elected by the citizens of this State, who are elected to serve this State in the Congress of the United States of America, whether as a Senator or a Representative, shall immediately work together during their terms of office, and propose or maintain similar Bills, in both houses of Congress, calling for a Repeal of any part of any Federal Law that illegalizes Marijuana in the United States, and thereby give the Right to illegalize Marijuana exclusively to the jurisdiction of the individual States.

The proposed Bill shall include all the points of fact as described in this Law, such as the points of fact about who will actually be using Marijuana after all the Local Laws and Insurance Policies are in place, and such as the points of fact about all the Marijuana Issues that are Happening in Countries that do not prohibit Marijuana Use;

the Congresspersons of this State may also consult the Agency of Marijuana Statistics to get other Statistics of Marijuana Use to support their proposed Bill.

ANOTHER GOOD DAY WITH GOD

Whenever a Majority Vote in One of the Two Houses of the United States Congress Votes against the proposed Bill, then all the Senators or Representatives of this State, elected for their respective House of Congress, shall Propose the same Bill again to the appropriate House Committee, and shall continue proposing the same Bill to the appropriate House Committee, indefinitely, whenever a Majority Vote in that House of Congress Votes against the proposed Bill.

If any Federal Judge rules by Court Decision, that the Voters of this State do not have the Right to tell their Congresspersons what to Vote for or Against in the United States Congress, then the Congresspersons of this State shall indefinitely propose and vote for the impeachment and removal from office of that Federal Judge.

If any Congressperson of this State does not obey this Law, then any Grand Jury in this State may indict that person in a State Court, without any Statute of Limitations being imposed on the Court Case, and upon conviction, that Convicted person shall not be permitted to Apply for Employment for any office in and for this State, and shall also not be permitted to be an Employee of any State or Local Government in this State.

This Section of this State Law, shall remain in effect until all the Bills or Amendments, as described in this Section, are enacted to be a Law, as described in this Section, however, the parts of this Section that calls for an indictment of any Congressperson of this State who disobeys this State Law, and that calls for the Removal of Office of a Federal Judge, and that Prevents the Congresspersons of this State from Voting for any Bill Contrary to this Section and this State Law, shall remain in effect indefinitely.

The Congresspersons of this State shall also support any other Bill proposed by another State that accomplishes the same purpose of this Section.

The Congresspersons of this State shall also Vote against any Bill proposed in the United States Congress that contradicts the purpose of this Section or that contradicts any Laws enacted pursuant to this Section.

Section 2 of 17. Agency of Marijuana Statistics - creation.

The State Legislature, shall enact Laws that create and govern a State Agency called The State Agency of Marijuana Statistics.

The Agency shall consist of one or more persons that handles all aspects of the Collection of Literature about Marijuana.

Such literature shall include Domestic Literature, and when applicable, International Literature, about:

* the use of marijuana for medical and non-medical use;

* various policies and regulations enacted by various Government Agencies, Private Businesses, and Insurance Companies, pertaining to Marijuana Use;

* Marijuana statistics put together for this State and elsewhere, and other such Literature about Marijuana Use and statistics within the United States and in those Countries where Marijuana Use is Illegal or Legal.

All such literature obtained by the Agency shall be a public record, however, any particular portion of a record that contains legally protected private information, such as a protected Name, Home Address, or Social Security Number, shall be blocked from that portion of the record so as to prevent the protected private information from being released to the public.

When the State Legislature makes regulations governing the Agency of Marijuana Statistics, the State Legislature shall ensure that a Copy of all the Literature obtained by the Agency of Marijuana Statistics is, at a minimum, available to the public in electronic format, and in downloadable electronic format, free of charge, if the free distribution of the material is granted by the Owner, else the at-cost charge may be applied to the distribution of the Electronic Format;

if the Literature can not be reproduced in Electronic Format, or if permission by the Owner for free distribution is not granted, or when otherwise applicable, a Copy shall also made available to the Public in the available Format used, and the costs to the public shall not to exceed the costs incurred in buying, printing, copying, and shipping the Material;

for the purposes of getting permission by the Owner, permission is hereby granted by the State for the free distribution and reproduction of any Literature discussed in this Section that is owned by the State.

Section 3 of 17. Current Policies and Regulations prohibiting Marijuana Use not abolished.

This Law DOES NOT amend or abolish any Internal Policy already written and in use, by any State or Local Governmental Agency, Private Business, or any other Entity, in this State, that prohibits marijuana use by their employees, by people on the Public, or Private, property they manage, or by people they do business with, however, sufficient signage must be posted when the Internal Policy is applicable to Visitors, so as to give sufficient Notice to those Visitors in any Particular Location, however, in any particular situation, the Notice can always be given Verbally, or as a mailed or hand delivered Paper Notice.

L

Section 4 of 17. Cities, Towns, Communities, can prohibit Marijuana Use.

All City, Town, and Community Laws, prohibiting Marijuana use, are nullified at the enactment of this Law, unless they were enacted with a 70% majority vote of the Voters;

and if nullified pursuant to this Section, any Local City, Town, or Local Community within this State, by a minimum 70% majority vote of the Voters therein, may adopt Uniform Local Laws and Uniform Community Regulations that completely or partially Prohibits any or all Private or Commercial use of marijuana within the Jurisdiction of any or all parts of their City, Town, or Community, including their roads, provided that any such Prohibitive Laws will not be valid in any particular situation, unless sufficient signage was posted to give sufficient notice to its Citizens and its Visitors in any Particular Location, however, in any particular situation, the Notice can always be given Verbally, or as a mailed or hand delivered Paper Notice.

Section 5 of 17. Counties can govern Marijuana Use.

All County Laws, prohibiting Marijuana use, are hereby nullified, unless they were enacted with a minimum 70% majority vote of the Voters, and after being nullified, any County, by a 70% or more majority vote of the voters therein, may adopt Uniform Local Laws that completely or partially prohibits any or all Private or Commercial use of marijuana within the Jurisdiction of their County, that is, or is not, within the jurisdiction of a City, Town, or Community, including their County roads, provided that any such Prohibitive Laws will not be valid in any particular situation, unless sufficient signage was posted to give sufficient notice to its Citizens and its Visitors in that situation, however, in any particular situation, the Notice can always be given Verbally, or as a mailed or hand delivered Paper Notice.

L

Section 6 of 17. Violators of Marijuana Use must also be filed with the Agency of Marijuana Statistics.

To the extent allowed by Law, all violations of marijuana use, including violations in Government Agencies, and Private Businesses, and all the results of urine samples acquired by those Places, including Insurance Companies and Hospitals, shall be filed with the Agency of Marijuana Statistics.

To the extent allowed by Law, all other miscellaneous statistics and information put together by Government Agencies in this State pertaining to Marijuana Use must also be filed with the Agency of Marijuana Statistics;

The Agency of Marijuana Statistics shall also accept all other miscellaneous statistics and information put together and offered voluntarily by Insurance Companies, Hospitals, and other Private Businesses, pertaining to the Use/Non-Use of Marijuana within this State or elsewhere.

Section 7 of 17. Age Limit of Marijuana Use to be 21, unless different age proposed.

The Private or Commercial manufacture, sale, consumption, or transportation of marijuana within this State, is prohibited from persons younger than 21 years of age, however, a higher or lower age, can be "not prohibited" by a Local Law enacted with a minimum 51% majority vote.

For the Purposes of this Law, The State Minimum Age Law, or if enacted, the Local Minimum Age Laws, and other State and Local Laws pertaining to Marijuana Use, always supersede Community Laws and Internal Policies, pertaining to higher Age Limits of Marijuana Use, and pertaining to other more restrictive prohibitions of Marijuana Use as enacted by any County and City pursuant to this Law.

L

Persons with Medical Prescriptions prescribing Marijuana Use are exempt from the State Age Limit;

the Age Limits of Marijuana Use by persons with a Medical Prescription prescribing such use, shall be prohibited according to Local Law or Internal Policy.

Section 8 of 17. Marijuana Use may be used against you in a Court of Law.

The State Legislature and Local Governments may enact Laws pertaining to methods and time limits, pertaining to collecting urine samples of persons involved in Automobile Accidents.

All persons involved in an Automobile Accident, or other type of accident as specified by State Law or Local Law or Internal Policy, will be required to submit a urine sample as directed by Law or Policy, to any Local Law Enforcement Agency, or to another Party as specified by Law or Policy, only if such Law Enforcement Agency or any Party involved in the collision requests that urine samples be acquired, or if Law or Policy otherwise requires urine samples to be acquired.

When an injury is alleged to be caused by another person, the results of all urine samples collected will be given to all the parties involved in the collision or accident upon request of a party involved, so as to enable the results to be used in a Court of Law, and a Refusal to give a urine sample, may also be used against a person in a Court of Law.

For all intents and purposes of this Section, only a Jury who has used Marijuana can be called to Answer a Question of Fact in a Court Case pertaining to the extent of liability against a person who was under the influence of Marijuana, during a Motor Vehicle Accident or other Accident, however, any Jury may be called for a Court Case if all the parties in the Accident refused to give a Urine Sample as described in this Section, or if the Jury is in a Jurisdiction that prohibits Marijuana Use.

The State Legislature or Local Governments may enact Laws pertaining to giving Written Tests to persons who are obtaining their Driver License, to ask the Applicants Questions about how the use of Marijuana may effect operating a Motor Vehicle, and about how the Local Laws and Internal Policies pertaining to Marijuana Use, and how the punishments for violations of those Laws and Policies, will vary in different Jurisdictions and on different properties.

L

Section 9 of 17. Marijuana Use can not be prohibited by State Law; State Legislature to enact uniform Laws pertaining to format of Prohibitive Signage used in State.

The State Legislature can not prohibit the Private or Commercial manufacture, sale, use, or transportation of marijuana, within this State, unless such State Law is directed towards State Government Employees;

for the purposes of this Section, the State Legislature may determine what constitutes a State Government Employee.

The Private or Commercial manufacture, sale, use, or transportation of marijuana, within this State may only be prohibited by Local Law and Internal Policies.

Nothing in this Law prevents the State Legislature to otherwise Regulate Marijuana Use, pursuant to General State Laws, pertaining to Violations of food quality, weights and measures, et cetera.

The State Legislature shall have the exclusive Right to enact Prohibitive Signage Laws to be used Uniformly throughout the State, pertaining to size, shape, wording, format, and placement, of Prohibitive Signs used in this State pertaining to Marijuana Use, whenever a State or Local Government Agency, or any other Public or Private Entity, wants to Give Public Notice to Visitors and others, as to Marijuana Prohibitions in their Jurisdiction or on their Property, however, this Section does not prevent an informal Prohibitive Sign from being used, and whenever an informal Prohibitive Sign is used at any particular Location, it will then be at the discretion of any particular Court or Jury to accept a claim that Sufficient Notice was Given.

For the purposes of this Law, all Uniform Local Laws and Uniform Community Regulations enacted pursuant to this Law that prohibits any Aspect of Marijuana Use within their Jurisdiction, shall be worded so as to "prohibit"any particular Aspect of Marijuana Use, and not worded so as to "Legalize" any particular Aspect of Marijuana Use, so as to not contradict a Federal Law, because as soon as the word "Legalized" is used, it may contradict a Federal Law.

L

For the purposes of this Law, all the Uniform Local Laws, Uniform Local Regulations, and Internal Policies enacted pursuant to this Law, that prohibits any particular aspect of Marijuana Use, shall also be filed with the Agency of Marijuana Statistics, to the extent allowed by Law.

For the purposes of this Law, the term "Majority Vote" used throughout this Law, means the Majority Vote of the Voters, and not the Majority Vote of the Elected or Appointed Government Legislature.

Section 10 of 17. Importation of Marijuana into this State prohibited - exception.

The Importation of marijuana, from another State, Foreign Country, or elsewhere, into any County, City, or Town, in this State, is prohibited unless specifically "not prohibited" according to Local Law of the appropriate County, City, or Town, by a minimum 70% majority vote;

and all such Importation, shall originate from, and be transported through, Locations that do not prohibit the Exportation and Transportation of Marijuana.

The State Legislature may enact State Laws that ensure that all Importation of Marijuana into this State, is done only from, through, and to Locations, where Exportation, Transportation, and Importation, of Marijuana is not prohibited.

Section 11 of 17. Exportation of Marijuana from this State not prohibited - exception.

The Exportation of marijuana from this State, for Private or Commercial use, through or to, any other State in the United States, or Foreign Government, or elsewhere, in violation of their Laws, is prohibited.

The State Legislature and Local Governments may enact Laws to prosecute Violators of this Section.

Section 12 of 17. Taxation not allowed unless Marijuana Legal.

Until the Congressional Federal Marijuana Laws, that prohibit the States from governing marijuana use within their State jurisdictions are repealed, this Section prevents all State and Local Governments within this State from taxing the manufacture, sale, consumption, or transportation of marijuana, so as to not be a party to any violation of a Federal Marijuana Law.

Nothing in this Section shall prevent the Agency of Marijuana Statistics from receiving statistics, about marijuana being Privately and Commercially manufactured, sold, consumed, or transported, in this State.

When the Federal Marijuana Laws allow this State to regulate marijuana use in this State, then taxation of Marijuana, if done, shall consider both the Food and Non-Food aspects of Marijuana use, and any such Taxation may be proposed by the State Legislature, or Local Governments, however, any State or Local Taxation of Marijuana in this State shall first be approved of by the Voters of this State.

Section 13 of 17. Federal Marijuana Laws not to be enforced - exceptions.

To the Extent allowed by any Federal Law, or to the Extent allowed by any Local County, City or Town Law, that was Enacted with a minimum 70% majority vote, or to the Extent allowed by Internal Policy not superseded by a Local Law, all Federal Laws prohibiting marijuana use in this State, will not be enforced by any State or Local Governmental Agency.

**Section 14 of 17. Effective Date of Law;
___2___ year waiting period before State Laws
prohibiting Marijuana Use in this State
voided;**

Waiting period to be used by Local Governments to
enact their prohibitive Laws.

All parts of this Law are effective at the Time this
Law is enacted by the Voters, except, all State
Laws prohibiting Marijuana Use will continue to
be in effect until the Next General Election, so as
to allow all the Counties and Cities and Towns in
this State, to prohibit any Aspect of Marijuana Use
in their Jurisdictions, if desired, as Described in
this Law, by a Minimum 70% Majority Vote, or
51% Majority Vote in the case of Age Limits;

Such prohibitive Laws can be proposed to the
Voters by the Voters themselves, or by their
Government Legislatures.

L

At the Next General Election, all State Laws in
this State that prohibit Marijuana Use, will be
Void, and the Right to Prohibit Marijuana Use will
be transferred to the Local Governments, as
described in this Law.

After this Law is enacted, the Local Governments have ___2___ years to enact any Prohibitive Marijuana Laws they want to enact,if any, in and for their Jurisdictions, before this Law Voids all the applicable Provisions of all State Laws that prohibit Marijuana Use in this State.

For the purposes of this Law, a County Law may be worded to supersede a less stringent City Law, Town Law, Internal Policy, or Community Law, and a City Law or Town Law may be worded to supersede a less stringent Internal Policy or Community Law, pertaining to Prohibiting and Regulating Marijuana Use in their Regulatory Jurisdictions.

Section 15 of 17. Amending and Interpreting this State Law.

(Put Chapter 4 here - the Interpretation Clause)

Section 16 of 17. Severibility of this Law.

If any part of this Law is held to be Invalid by a Government Court or a Government Legislature, because of a conflict with another Law that supersedes this Law, then that part of this Law may be deemed to be temporarily unenforceable, and the other parts of this Law shall remain Effective for their Intents and Purposes.

This is a State Law, and as such, any provision of this Law that conflicts with any provision of a State Constitutional Law pertaining to Marijuana Use will be Void.

Section 17 of 17. Paying the Bill.

(Put Chapter 5 here - the Reimbursement Clause)

* * * *

L

M

Example Petition:

**US Government
not allowed
to Spy**

M

US Constitutional Law

(free to copy and modify)

Preamble of the Law.

Spying is Stealing.

This Law prevents the US Executive Department from spying on Foreigners, or others, in times of peace.

We the People thank GOD for this Law.

PART A. SPYING ON FOREIGNERS.

Section 1 of 2. US Government not allowed to spy in Times of Peace.

The US Government and the Several States thereof, and any employee thereof, is not allowed to spy on any Foreign Government, or any other individual or groups of individuals Foreign or Not, when a War is not officially declared by the US Congress against those persons.

M

The US Congress shall enact Public Laws that describe what activities shall be jointly considered Illegal spying, when done by or to the United States in violation of this Amendment, and what activities shall be jointly considered Legal spying, when done by or to the United States and that would be permitted by anyone.

Section 2 of 2. Interpretation of this Law by the US Congress.

If any part of this Law needs Interpretation by a Federal Court in the United States, after any part of this Law is enacted to be an Amendment to the US Constitution, then such an Interpretation shall be asked to be done by the US Congress, and shall not be done by any Federal Court in the United States;

the US Congress may then, at the Discretion of the US Congress, ask the Voters of the United States for the Interpretation.

PART B. DUTIES OF CONGRESSPERSONS OF THIS STATE; INTERPRETATION OF THIS STATE LAW; AMENDMENTS; PAYING THE PROPONENT OF THIS LAW.

Section 1 of 3. Duties of this State's Congresspersons.

Each person elected by the citizens of this State, who are elected to serve this State in the Congress of the United States of America, whether as a Senator or a Representative, shall immediately work together during their terms of office, and propose or maintain similar Bills, in both houses of Congress, calling for an Amendment to the United States Constitution that includes all the text included in Part A of this Law.

(Put the remainder of Chapter 3 here - the Control Your Congress Clause)

M

Section 2 of 3. Amending and Interpreting this State Law.

(Put Chapter 4 here - the Interpretation Clause)

Section 3 of 3. Paying the Bill.

(Put Chapter 5 here - the Reimbursement Clause)

* * * *

N

Example Petition:

Liberating Germany

N

Federal Law

(free to copy and modify)

Preamble of the Law.

Many Historians, Holocaust Scholars, and Holocaust Deniers have provided much recent evidence about who Hitler really was, and why so many countries were doing a World War 1 and World War 2 (a.k.a World War 1 part 2) against Germany and Hitler.

The recent historical evidence that has been provided contradicts much of the propaganda that is put into domestic hollywood movies and domestic news tabloids, both dominated by gypsy jews.

As a result of the conflicting historical evidence, and the staggering amount of US tax payer money being paid to fund unnecessary US military bases in Germany, this Law forces the US government to withdraw all US military from Germany.

N

We the People thank GOD for this Law.

PART A. US MILITARY MUST BE REMOVE FROM GERMANY

Section 1 of 1. All US military must be vacate Germany.

All the US military buildings inside Germany owned by US Government shall be demolished, and the resulting garbage shall be disposed of to a location inside of Germany or outside of Germany, as decided by the German Government, and all the expenses of the demolition and garbage removal shall be paid for by the US Executive Department within the current allocated budget of the US Executive Department; the buildings shall be demolished and disposed of within ___4___ years after this Law is enacted to be a US Law.

After the buildings are disposed of, the US military shall completely depart Germany within ___1___ year.

PART B. US CONGRESS TO REPEAL ALL POST WAR US LAWS AND SANCTIONS AGAINST GERMANY.

Section 1 of 1. US Congress must repeal all post war US Laws and sanctions against Germany that resulted as a direct result of WW1 and WW2.

The US Congress must repeal all post war US Laws and sanctions against Germany that resulted as a direct result of WW1 and WW2.

N

PART C. DUTIES OF CONGRESSPERSONS OF THIS STATE; INTERPRETATION OF THIS LAW; PAYING THE PROPONENT OF THIS LAW.

Section 1 of 5. Duties of this State's Congresspersons.

Each person elected by the citizens of this State, who are elected to serve this State in the Congress of the United States of America, whether as a Senator or a Representative, shall immediately work together during their terms of office, and propose or maintain similar Bills, in both houses of Congress, calling for a Federal Law that includes all the Text included in Part A and Part B of this Law.

(Put the remainder of Chapter 3 here - the Control Your Congress Clause)

Section 2 of 5. Amending and Interpreting this State Law (after enacted as a State Law).

(Put Chapter 4 here - the Interpretation Clause)

Section 3 of 5. Interpretation of this US Law (after enacted as a US Law).

If any part of this Law needs Interpretation by a Federal Court in the United States, after any part of this Law is enacted to be a US Law, then such an Interpretation shall be asked to be done by the US Congress, and shall not be done by any Federal Court in the United States;

the US Congress may then, at the Discretion of the US Congress, ask the Voters of the United States for the Interpretation.

Section 4 of 5. Stopping Funds to US Executive Department for failure to comply (after enacted as a State Law).

The US Congress shall stop all funding to the US Executive Department when the US Executive Department is not fully complying with this law.

N

Section 5 of 5. Paying the Bill.

(Put Chapter 5 here - the Reimbursement Clause)

* * * *

Example Petition:

emancipated negroes eligible for free ticket back to africa

State and Federal Law

(free to copy and modify)

Preamble of the Law.

After the Civil War, lobbyists and the United States Government created Liberia Africa for Emancipated negroes to return to, although, the United States Government failed to provide any transportation for those Impoverished, Emancipated negroes, to get there.

This State Law provides a Free, One-Way, Airfare ticket, to any negroe to get to Liberia Africa, and asks the United States Congress to provide the same, and also asks the United States Congress to reimburse this State for any Free Tickets thus far provided.

It should also be noted that the official Language of Liberia Africa, is the English Language, the same Language spoken in the United States, and therefore, the transition of returning to Africa will be easier for any negroe who returns to Africa.

We the People thank GOD for this Law.

Section 1 of 5. Free Ticket to Africa for emancipated negroes.

The State Legislature shall enact State Laws to fund a General Fund, that pays for one Free, One-Way Airfare Ticket, to any negroe in this State who wants to travel to Liberia Africa.

Section 2 of 5. Time for State Legislature to enact State Laws.

Pursuant to this Law, the State Legislature shall enact all the required State Laws, according to this Law, before the next General Election.

Section 3 of 5. Duties of State's Congresspersons.

Each person elected by the citizens of this State, who are elected to serve this State in the Congress of the United States of America, whether as a Senator or a Representative, shall immediately work together during their terms of office, and propose or maintain similar Bills, in both houses of Congress, calling for a Federal Law, substantially similar to Section 1 of this Law, and that also Refunds this State, and any other State, for any moneys thus far spent in Transporting negroes to Liberia Africa pursuant to this Law.

(Put the remainder of Chapter 3 here - the Control Your Congress Clause)

Section 4 of 5. Amending and Interpreting this State Law.

(Put Chapter 4 here - the Interpretation Clause)

Section 5 of 5. Paying the Bill.

(Put Chapter 5 here - the Reimbursement Clause)

* * * *

P

Example Petition:

**imprisoned negroes
eligible for free ticket
back to africa
after imprisoned
half-sentence**

State and Federal Law

P

ANOTHER GOOD DAY WITH GOD

(free to copy and modify)

Preamble of the Law.

This Law reduces prison over crowding.

It should be noted that this Law does not free any imprisoned negroe;

this Law simply relocates imprisoned negroes to Liberia Africa, after the negroes serve half of their sentence in this State, and then releases them in Liberia Africa if they renounce their United States Citizenship and agree to be transported to Liberia Africa.

It should also be noted that the United States Government made Liberia Africa, specifically for emancipated negroes after the Civil War, and that the Official Language of Liberia Africa is the English Language.

P

We the People thank GOD for this Law.

Section 1 of 4. negroes to be given choice to return to Liberia Africa after serving half of their jail term.

Any negroe imprisoned in any State or Local Jail or Prison in this State, for any amount of time, after serving half their sentence, shall be asked if they want to be transported to Liberia Africa and given an early release in Liberia Africa if they voluntarily renounce their United States Citizenship.

Section 2 of 4. Duties of State Legislature.

The State Legislature shall enact all the necessary State Laws, to regulate this Law, before the next General Election, and upon such enactment, this Law will become effective.

Section 3 of 4. Amending and Interpreting this State Law.

(Put Chapter 4 here - the Interpretation Clause)

Section 4 of 4. Paying the Bill.

(Put Chapter 5 here - the Reimbursement Clause)

* * * *

Q

Other Suggested Initiative Petitions

Q

APPENDIX :
EXAMPLE PETITIONS

1 State Congresspersons must petition this US Constitutional Amendment to US Congress to **Raise Voting Age to __47__**

2 State Law to mandate that **all Voter Ballots must be paper Ballots, and can be sorted electronically, but must be counted manually**

3 State Congresspersons must petition this US Constitutional Amendment to US Congress to **Define Marriage**

4 State Congresspersons must petition this Federal Law to US Congress to **Abolish the Federal Reserve Act of 1913**

5 State Congresspersons must petition this Federal Law to US Congress to **Abolish the IRS and Establish a Flat Tax**

☿

6 State/Federal Laws to mandate that all **Public Restrooms and Public Shower-rooms must be single-person**

7 State Congresspersons must petition this Federal Law to US Congress to **Give each Prisoner at Guantanamo Bay a Speedy Public Court Trial, with Public or Private Defender, Court Appeals, and Compensation if Acquitted**

8 State Congresspersons must petition this Federal Law to US Congress to **Abolish Federally Mandated Health Care**

9 **Abortion**

10 State Law to **Regulate Gasoline Prices**

11 State and/or Federal Laws to **Set the State and the Federal Tax Rates**

12 State/Federal Laws to **Set the Salary Rates for State/Federal Government Employees**

13 State Congresspersons must petition this Federal Law to US Congress to **Prevent the Federal NSA and all other Federal Agencies from performing any warrantless collection and warrantless searches of private information owned by domestic civilians and foreigners**

14 State Congresspersons must petition this Federal Law to US Congress to **Legalize Statewide Initiative Petitions in all States**

☿

R

Memorandum from California Secretary of State,

that prevents Electronic Signatures (only on Initiative Petitions)

R

ANOTHER GOOD DAY WITH GOD

(Page 1 of 2)

DEBRA BOWEN | SECRETARY OF STATE
STATE OF CALIFORNIA | ELECTIONS
1500 11th Street, 5th Floor | Sacramento, CA 95814 | Tel (916) 657-2166 | Fax (916) 653-3214 | www.sos.ca.gov

February 9, 2010

County Clerk/Registrar of Voters (CC/ROV) Memorandum # 10063

TO: All County Clerks/Registrars of Voters

FROM: _Cathy Mitchell_
          Cathy Mitchell
          Chief, Elections Division

RE: Initiative: Petition Signatures

Recently, the Secretary of State's office learned that one or more counties have been or may soon be presented with initiative petitions, or electronic devices that are represented as containing initiative petitions, purportedly signed by California voters.

These particular "petitions" raise a new issue in that they purportedly were presented to the voter in an electronic format and the voter was asked to provide a signature, printed name, and residence address using their finger on the screen of a personal electronic device instead of using a pen to write those items on a paper petition. The electronic documents containing the images of the voter's information have been or may soon be provided electronically, or converted to paper and presented, to the county elections office for acceptance.

After carefully considering the issue, the Secretary of State's office has concluded that documents circulated and information gathered in the above manner are not valid under current law and may not be accepted by an elections official.

The California Constitution – Article II, Section 10(e) – reads:

> The Legislature shall provide the manner in which petitions shall be circulated, presented, and certified, and measures submitted to the electors.

ANOTHER GOOD DAY WITH GOD

(Page 2 of 2)

The Legislature has set forth numerous requirements for those who circulate petitions and for elections officials who must determine whether the petitions comply with the law and the Constitution. None of the petition circulation requirements enacted by the Legislature mention electronically gathering the information required by statute to be placed on the petition. There is also nothing to suggest that the Legislature contemplated the use of this technology in establishing the legal framework for the circulation of election petitions.

One requirement is found in Elections Code section 100, which reads in part:

> Each signer shall at the time of signing the petition or paper **personally affix** his or her signature, printed name, and place of residence, giving street and number, and if no street or number exists, then a designation of the place of residence which will enable the location to be readily ascertained. (Emphasis added.)

Even if a voter can personally enter their required information into a personal electronic device, that personal electronic device is not the petition itself and it is not what is provided to an elections official. What is or will be provided, either electronically or on paper, to an elections official is a facsimile of the required information that each voter, by law, must personally affix to a petition. Submitting a facsimile of the information required to be collected and personally affixed by EC 100 does not comply with the law.

If the Legislature and the Governor wish to accommodate a new form of technology, a change in law is necessary. Any such change in this area will undoubtedly raise complex public policy questions involving security, privacy and budgetary issues that will need to be resolved.

If you have any questions, please feel free to contact me at Cathy.Mitchell@sos.ca.gov or (916) 657-2166.

R

273

S

Personal Letter
sent to

Caifornia Governor
Jerry Brown

about Legalizing
Initiative Petitions

(Oct 2011)

S

(Page 1 of 3) Letter to Jerry Brown.

```
DATE SENT:             October 1, 2011
NEXT GENERAL ELECTION:  November 2012


TO:

Governor Jerry Brown
RE: Big 5 Capacity
RE: Proposed Law
c/o State Capitol, Suite 1173
Sacramento, CA 95814


FROM:

██████████
████████████


RE:

Proposed Law:
THE ELECTRONIC SIGNATURE LAW, FOR INITIATIVE PETITIONS


NOTE:

This Letter has also been sent to the other 4 members of the big 5.

I request that you review this Letter before your next big 5 meeting.

I also request that you give this Law a certain amount of Precedence above other
Proposed Laws that are currently before the California Legislature.
```

ANOTHER GOOD DAY WITH GOD

(Page 2 of 3) Letter to Jerry Brown.

In this Letter, I Request that you (in your big 5 capacity), Enact a State Law that allows Initiative Petitions to be signed Online using Electronic Signatures.

Below is the Text of the proposed Law. I am hoping that the proposed Law can be presented to both Legislative Houses, simultaneously, and be passed before the Next General Election, to allow Initiative Petitions to be signed Online at least 5 months before the 2012 General Election.

THE ELECTRONIC SIGNATURE LAW, FOR INITIATIVE PETITIONS

1. Only the [Secretary of State] is allowed to maintain an Online Site for the purposes Collecting Electronic Signatures Online for Initiative Petitions that are approved for Circulation Statewide or Locally; the [Secretary of State], or the appropriate Local Government Clerks, shall also ensure that all Statewide or Local Initiative Petitions approved for Circulation are posted Online at the Site.

2. Within 2 months after the Enactment of this Law, the [Secretary of State] shall initiate a functioning Online Site, to accomplish the purposes of this Law; the Online Site must at a minimum:
(a) be accessible by all the appropriate Government Clerks, for the purposes of allowing the Clerks to Validate the Electronic Signatures of the persons Residing in their Jurisdictions, and also for the purposes of allowing the Clerks to Post any Locally Circulated Initiative Petitions at the Site, and,
(b) allow Registered Voters to use a Username and Password to sign-in, after providing sufficient Personal Information to register at the Site, for the purposes of signing and un-signing Initiative Petitions Online at the Site.

Brief History
of
Electronic Signatures on Initiative Petitions.

In recent years, the whole Issue of Electronic Signatures on Initiative Petitions has been discussed many times in the California Government. The only thing that seems to be preventing the Issue from being resolved, is that the discussions were entirely limited to the Risks of letting the Public Circulators Collect Electronic Signatures. The discussions never introduced the possibility that the Secretary of State would be the person Collecting the Electronic Signatures. And as such, this entire discussion just seems to continue and continue without resolution, until now. With the above Law, ONLY THE [SECRETARY OF STATE] CAN COLLECT ELECTRONIC SIGNATURES, and therefore, ALL THE NECESSARY SAFEGUARDS CAN BE EASILY REGULATED.

It should also be noted, that the California Legislature has already Enacted many California Codes that allow the California Government to accept many different types of Signatures, including Electronic Signatures. But somehow, Initiative Petitions got to be specifically excluded from those Codes, pursuant to Agency Memorandums and such, but once again, those Memorandums were looking at the Circulators, not the [Secretary of State], as the person who would be Collecting the Electronic Signatures.

It should also be noted that the Proposed Law above can be used as part of any Re-Election Campaign, because: (1) this Law is "Environmentally Green", saving 70+/- reams of paper per Petition and other environmental costs pertaining to Circulating Initiative Petitions. (2) this Law makes it easier for the California People to Propose and Sign Initiative Petitions. (3) I will not have to tell the California People that you Refused to Enact this Proposed Law Yourselves - I would tell them about your Refusal in the Preamble of My Own Initiative Petition for this Law.

Thanks. From, ████████████████████████ - Look For God.

S

(Page 3 of 3) Copies of the Letter were mailed to the following five government officials in California.

```
Governor Jerry Brown
RE: Big 5 Capacity
RE: Proposed Law
c/o State Capitol, Suite 1173
Sacramento, CA 95814


President pro Tempore,
Darrell Steinberg
RE: Big 5 Capacity
RE: Proposed Law
District Office
1020 N Street, Room 576
Sacramento, CA 95814


Minority Leader,
Senator Robert D. Dutton
RE: Big 5 Capacity
RE: Proposed Law
Rancho Cucamonga Office
8577 Haven Avenue, Suite 210
Rancho Cucamonga, CA 91730


Assembly Speaker,
John A. Perez
RE: Big 5 Capacity
RE: Proposed Law
320 West 4th Street
Room 1050
Los Angeles, CA 90013


Assembly Minority Leader,
Connie Conway
RE: Big 5 Capacity
RE: Proposed Law
District Office
113 N. Church St., Suite 505
Visalia, CA 93291
```

No Response has yet been received.

T

List of States
that allow
Initiative Petitions

T

The abbreviations below (C,S,P,c,s), correspond to the abbreviations used in the table below.

C **Direct** Initiative Petition: for *State Constitutional Amendment* - The Voters can do an Initiative Petition to put a proposed State Constitutional Amendment onto their State Ballot.

Permitted in the following States:

Arizona, Arkansas, California, Colorado, Florida, Illinois, Michigan, Missouri, Montana, Nebraska, Nevada, North Dakota, Ohio, Oklahoma, Oregon, South Dakota.

S **Direct** Initiative Petition: for *State Law* - The Voters can do an Initiative Petition to put a proposed State Law onto their State Ballot.

Permitted in the following States:

Alaska, Arizona, Arkansas, California, Colorado, Idaho, Missouri, Montana, Nebraska, North Dakota, Oklahoma, Oregon, South Dakota, Utah, Washington, Wyoming.

P **Popular** Referendum - The Voters can do an Initiative Petition to put a State Law enacted by the State Legislature onto their State Ballot.

Permitted in the following States:

Alaska, Arizona, Arkansas, California, Colorado, Idaho, Kentucky, Maine, Maryland, Massachusetts, Michigan, Missouri, Montana, Nebraska, Nevada, New Mexico, North Dakota, Ohio, Oklahoma, Oregon, South Dakota, Utah, Washington, Wyoming.

T

C **Indirect** Initiative Petition: for *State Constitutional Amendment* - The Voters can do an Initiative Petition, to ask their State Legislature to put a proposed State Constitutional Amendment onto their State Ballot.

Permitted in the following States:

Massachusetts, Mississippi.

S **Indirect** Initiative Petition: for *State Law* - The Voters can do an Initiative Petition, to ask their State Legislature to put a proposed State Law onto their State Ballot.

Permitted in the following States:

Maine, Massachusetts, Michigan, Nevada, Ohio, Utah, Washington.

ANOTHER GOOD DAY WITH GOD

Table of States that allow some type of Initiative Petition

1	AK	Alaska		S	P		
2	AZ	Arizona	C	S	P		
3	AR	Arkansas	C	S	P		
4	CA	California	C	S	P		
5	CO	Colorado	C	S	P		
6	FL	Florida	C				
7	ID	Idaho		S	P		
8	IL	Illinois	C				
9	KY	Kentucky			P		
10	ME	Maine			P		s
11	MD	Maryland			P		
12	MA	Massachusetts			P	c	s
13	MI	Michigan	C		P		s
14	MS	Mississippi				c	

(See previous pages for meaning of "C", "S", "P", "c", and "s")

T

(Continued from Previous Page)

15	MO	Missouri	C	S	P		
16	MT	Montana	C	S	P		
17	NE	Nebraska	C	S	P		
18	NV	Nevada	C		P		s
19	NM	New Mexico			P		
20	ND	North Dakota	C	S	P		
21	OH	Ohio	C		P		s
22	OK	Oklahoma	C	S	P		
23	OR	Oregon	C	S	P		
24	SD	South Dakota	C	S	P		
25	UT	Utah		S	P		s
26	WA	Washington		S	P		s
27	WY	Wyoming		S	P		
		Totals	**21**	24	2	7	

(See previous pages for meaning of "C", "S", "P", "c", and "s")